Finance of International Trade

Essential Capital Markets

Finance of International Trade

Eric Bishop

ELSEVIER
BUTTERWORTH
HEINEMANN

AMSTERDAM BOSTON HEIDELBERG LONDON NEW YORK OXFORD
PARIS SAN DIEGO SAN FRANCISCO SINGAPORE SYDNEY TOKYO

Butterworth-Heinemann is an imprint of Elsevier
Linacre House, Jordan Hill, Oxford OX2 8DP, UK
30 Corporate Drive, Suite 400, Burlington, MA 01803, USA

First edition 2004
Reprinted 2006, 2008

Notice
No responsibility is assumed by the publisher for any injury and/or damage to persons
or property as a matter of products liability, negligence or otherwise, or from any use
or operation of any methods, products, instructions or ideas contained in the material
herein. Because of rapid advances in the medical sciences, in particular, independent
verification of diagnoses and drug dosages should be made

British Library Cataloguing in Publication Data
—A catalogue record for this book is available from the British Library

Library of Congress Cataloging-in-Publication Data
A catalog record for this book is available from the Library of Congress

ISBN: 978-0-7506-5908-6

For information on all Butterworth-Heinemann publications
visit our website at books.elsevier.com

08 09 10 10 9

Working together to grow
libraries in developing countries

www.elsevier.com | www.bookaid.org | www.sabre.org

ELSEVIER   BOOK AID
International   Sabre Foundation

Transferred to Digital Printing 2009

Contents

Preface

Countries world-wide have traded among themselves for over 2000 years using wide-ranging methods of settlement. Exporters of goods naturally seek security of payment, whereas importers endeavour to ensure that they receive precisely those goods they have contracted to buy and for which they insist on correct documentation for customs clearance purposes.

Raw materials, oil, liquid gas, coal, manufactured goods, soft commodities, fresh and frozen foods all form just a part of the vast quantities of freight being carried every day by air, sea, road, rail and inland waterways. To those must be added the export of technology and industrial and manufacturing systems for the introduction and modernization of industry in less-developed and third world countries.

Advances in technology have improved transport by sea and air enabling carriers to move goods with ever-increasing speed and safety. When an importer and exporter enter into a contract to buy and sell goods they set in motion a series of activities involving numerous support services provided by forwarding agents, road transporters, railway operators, shipping companies, banks and insurers; each is an important link in the movement of goods from one country to another. The principal operators in international trade combine their respective skills to ensure the successful completion of transactions and the reduction or elimination of those risks which are ever-present in cross-border trading.

Depending upon their relationships with one another, some traders may be prepared to deal on **open account** where the exporter despatches goods and documents direct to his buyer and awaits payment in due course. However, where levels of experience are less well-established, exporters can select a method of settlement in keeping with their specific requirements.

Most international trade transactions are financed at some point, principally by banks specializing in this activity, particularly in protecting against risk during all stages of transport up to final destination.

For the exporter, those risks are non-payment or late payment which both seriously affect cash flow. The importer, on the other hand, faces the risks of non-delivery, short delivery and delivery of substandard goods.

In addition, where the importer or buyer is on-selling the relative goods to a foreign buyer, he runs the risk that incorrect or faulty documents from the overseas supplier may be rejected at final destination.

Those specializing in finance have devised a range of products and techniques to provide trade operators with varying degrees of protection against commercial and financial risks and to ensure settlement of contracts.

The **bill for collection** is by far the most widely used and relatively inexpensive method of settlement. It involves the exporter in despatching his goods, raising the documents and handing them, together with a bill of exchange, to his bank for collection. The documents are then sent to a foreign bank for payment or acceptance by the buyer.

This method is not without risk, for if the importer fails to pay or accept the bill of exchange, the exporter's goods may be left stranded in a foreign port. Although there are certain facilities available with foreign banks to reduce the risk of non-payment, exporters who are reluctant to accept the risks involved in collections will opt to use the safest known method of settlement in international trade.

Known as the **irrevocable documentary credit** this instrument is capable of meeting the most stringent requirements of exporters and importers. It is a form of conditional guarantee issued by a bank which ensures that the beneficiary (exporter) will be paid for his goods if he ships them and raises correct documents. For the buyer (importer) the irrevocable credit provides a guarantee that the exporter will only be paid when he has actually despatched the goods and presented correct documents to the negotiating bank.

Since its inception over 150 years ago, this instrument has undergone considerable change and adaptation. Available at sight, usance or on a deferred payment basis, it can be used to meet a whole range of situations and contractual obligations. We now have revolving, transferable, back-to-back, red clause, green clause, instalment and part payment credits; they are all designed to provide the exporter with some degree of pre-shipment finance and the importer with a level of discipline over shipment schedules and quality of goods.

Many transactions, although financed by traditional bank instruments and techniques, require the support of **on-demand guarantees** and **standby credits**. Both are issued by banks to support contracts for the supply and construction of major civil undertakings, such as airports, highways, bridges and industrial plant. They can be used in conjunction with documentary credits as a means of ensuring that exporters adhere to agreed shipment schedules and quality standards. Each instrument becomes dependent upon the other.

The issue and operation by banks throughout the world of instruments and techniques dealt with in this book are subject to a series of publications by the **International Chamber of Commerce, Paris** governing practice and providing operational recommendations.

They are:

- Incoterms 2000
- Uniform Rules for Collections
- Uniform Customs and Practice for Documentary Credits
- Uniform Rules for Bank to Bank Reimbursement under Documentary Credits

- Uniform Rules for On-Demand Guarantees
- International Standby Practices.

No trade transaction can be set in motion without some form of **marine insurance** to cover the risks inherent in transportation of goods. The **Institute of London Underwriters** has drawn up a wide range of clauses known as **Institute Cargo Clauses** to cover the movement of most manufactured goods, plus specific clauses for a variety of raw materials, frozen foods, commodities and dangerous cargoes.

To protect themselves against default by buyers and against political risks, such as intervention by foreign central banks to restrict or deny release of foreign exchange to pay for imports and the imposition of export and import embargoes, traders are able to take out **export credit insurance**. Most of the major trading nations have their own form of export credit insurance, in many cases with government funding; the incentive to exporters is obvious. As a consequence of using export credit insurance exporters are able to obtain finance at preferential rates by assigning their policies to the banks.

Beyond the traditional day-to-day operations in international trade we find two rather more complicated and technically sophisticated practices.

Forfaiting is a service offered by specialized operators, designed to enable exporters of plant, machinery and technology to enter markets which traditionally require long-term finance. The forfaiter buys from the exporter a series of bills of exchange or promissory notes, drawn on and accepted by the overseas buyer and guaranteed by an agreed local bank. For the exporter this method is particularly advantageous as the forfaiter discounts the bills completely without recourse. Bills discounted by forfaiters are traded in a secondary market to provide liquidity for the practice.

Countertrade is another specialist technique which can be used to assist countries with little or no foreign exchange to import goods without paying in currency. The importing countries may produce goods or raw materials which are not attractive to the overseas seller, but by finding a third country prepared to buy those goods or raw materials and pay in currency, the original exporter can be paid.

Many versions of countertrade have been developed whereby payment for exports is made by a combination of goods, services, currency and franchises. Apart from assisting cash-short countries to purchase essential goods, countertrade also enables exporters to find additional outlets for their products.

In line with the development of **e-commerce** a group of banks, carriers and insurers involved with international trade have developed an electronic system designed to speed up the movement of documents and methods of settlement. The system is known as **Bolero** and its application and advantages are dealt with in detail. It will have an undoubted impact on international trade, particularly in the prevention of fraud.

This book examines in depth the whole range of settlement methods for international trade, the risks involved, the contractual relationships between the parties and the relevant International Chamber of Commerce rules.

Chapter 1

Principal players

- Exporters
- Importers
- Freight forwarders
- Warehousemen
- Carriers
- Insurers
- Banks
- Factors
- Government agencies and international financial institutions

Exporters

Exporters are at the beginning of any international trade transaction and may be manufacturers, traders, farmers or commodity producers. They sell goods or services to overseas buyers in a variety of ways and, unless they are part of a large group, will almost certainly require the services of the other main players. Their aim is to get their goods to buyers around the world in the quickest and safest manner possible and to be paid in the correct currency and within their agreed terms of settlement.

The importance of exports to the economies of many countries is demonstrated by the wide range of support and encouragement given by governments, particularly through Export Credit Agencies (ECAs). These agencies offer facilities for promoting exports and allowing exporters to compete with overseas competitors who often enjoy the advantages of low-cost labour and raw materials. Multinational groups have spread their growth into these low-cost areas and their repatriated profits assist in reducing balance of payment deficits but, clearly, direct exporting has a greater impact and qualifies for as much assistance as can be afforded.

Countries with large surpluses of natural resources are heavily dependent upon exports, with the result that they are often obliged to enter into countertrade schemes with countries lacking foreign exchange, but requiring essential commodities. Countertrade is a specialized form of finance designed to facilitate trade between countries unable to earn foreign exchange to pay for imports and countries needing to find markets for their products.

Importers

Importers may equally be manufacturers buying raw materials for their factories, oil companies buying crude oil for refining, or simply merchants and traders fulfilling contracts with domestic and foreign consumers. For the latter, import finance is generally critical, often bridging the period between import and resale. Consequently, merchants and traders rely heavily on banks and warehousemen to whom they will pledge their goods before they are re-packed and transported to final buyers. It is important for them that their overseas suppliers are only paid when the goods ordered have actually been despatched; this involves the use of payment methods operated by banks, secured by title to the goods.

Although importers are not looked upon as favourably as exporters in countries with balance of trade problems, their contribution to the economy is valuable. Raw materials, foodstuffs, energy and services are essential to maintain industrial output where there are no natural resources and the resultant manufactured goods become exchange-earning exports. Sourcing their raw material requirements involves importers in scouring the world for quality, price and reliable delivery programmes. The spread of multinational groups has succeeded to some extent in ensuring supply from mineral-rich countries in which they have invested for import into other areas where they have a presence.

Traders and merchants import goods for resale and for processing before re-export. They also enter into contracts with foreign suppliers for goods which are consigned direct to buyers in other foreign countries. This is a highly skilled activity which demands extensive bridging finance to enable the operator to buy and sell at the most advantageous prices. Profits from trading and merchanting are made in foreign exchange and contribute to a country's reserves.

Freight forwarders

Freight forwarders, or forwarding agents as they are otherwise known, are probably the most versatile operators in the trade chain. They collect goods from exporters, sometimes actually packing them for shipment, transport them to ports of shipment by road, rail or barge and arrange with the shipping company (or airline) for them to be loaded on board. Their knowledge of overseas markets, the documentation required and the current import regulations applying in foreign countries is of great value to exporters who will often entrust them with the preparation of certain documents requiring chamber of commerce certification and consular legalisation. Of particular importance is the ability of freight forwarders to issue bills of lading covering goods during transport by several different means; these are known as multimodal bills of lading. Exporters may benefit from the freight forwarder combining their goods with those from other exporters and negotiating with the carrier for a bulk discount on the freight.

Warehousemen

Warehousemen perform a valuable service prior to the shipment of goods and after their arrival at the port of destination. As they are always holding goods belonging to a third party it is essential that they meet stringent security requirements, the most important of which is that they should be completely independent. Whenever finance is required for goods which have to be warehoused at some stage in a transaction, the bank will want to be certain that the warehouse company is completely trustworthy and properly managed. It will be expected to issue receipts, known as warehouse warrants, which can be negotiated to a third party when the person named in them wishes to transfer ownership of the goods. Before allowing goods to be stored in a particular warehouse, even though the requirements mentioned above have been satisfied, banks will examine the warehouse keeper's current insurance cover and endeavour to have their financial interest noted on the policy. Of particular value in warehousing facilities is the function of specialist packing. Warehousemen have an excellent knowledge of the type of packing required to protect goods during any form of transportation and to meet specific regulations in force in foreign countries.

Carriers

Goods may be transported in a number of different ways and by several types of carriers. We have dealt with freight forwarders who can handle goods through their journey via different modes of carriage and for which they issue multimodal transport documents. But there exists a need for independent **road hauliers**, **barge operators** and **railway companies** to carry goods on specific routes and to be responsible for the whole journey. Each provides an excellent service with the advantage that goods are only loaded and unloaded once. There is widespread use of **sealed containers** which are carried by trucks, barges and seagoing vessels, often containing goods from more than one exporter and consigned to various importers at destination.

Containers offer a number of advantages over traditional shipping practices. They are much larger than any other form of packing, are sealed and numbered in code by the carrier, can be carried on deck and are constructed to fit on to all forms of road and rail transport.

Shipping companies and **airlines** are by far the most important carriers who, between them, handle the greater part of all world trade. Major shipping lines operate scheduled services on specific routes while other carriers are free to accept cargoes for delivery anywhere in the world. Refrigerated vessels, bulk carriers, oil tankers and container vessels are only a few examples of how shipping lines cater for an infinite variety of commodities, perishable foodstuff, livestock, frozen products and manufactured goods. Banks and insurance companies now insist on limiting the age of vessels carrying goods in which they have an interest and are also cautious of vessels flying flags of convenience. These requirements tend to direct trade towards the established carriers with undoubted reputations. The practice of chartering vessels to carry specific cargoes to a destination of the charterer's choice has grown considerably, particularly in the transport of oil and liquid gases. The increased use of air freight to carry flowers, fruit, vegetables and other perishable goods has meant that producers can now sell in markets which are many thousands of miles away and know that the goods will still be fresh on arrival. Where speed is of the essence, exporters will always resort to air freight. Urgently required spare parts for power stations and desalination plants, for example, can be in place sometimes within a matter of hours, thereby minimizing production losses.

When shipping companies accept goods for shipment and load them on board, they hand the shipper a bill of lading. This document is negotiable by endorsement and enables any bank financing a transaction to obtain title to the goods as security. With airlines, however, the air consignment note which they issue is **not negotiable**, most consignments generally going direct to the importer. Banks dislike having goods consigned to their order for obvious reasons.

Insurers

Any movement of goods by sea, air or land transport involves certain hazards. However well a consignment is packed there is always the possibility of damage being incurred in transit; in some parts of the world, piracy and hijacking is prevalent. Most shipments are financed by banks or other finance institutions who want to ensure that their security, for that is what the goods generally are, is properly insured.

The major insurance groups provide a wide range of cover against marine and war risks, and in many cases write specific policies for individual commodities. For example, the risks involved in carrying a cargo of liquid gas are entirely different from those likely to arise when carrying wheat, sugar or frozen products. The value to banks of having shipments properly insured by established and undoubted insurance companies is paramount. They must be sure that their interest in the insurance cover has been noted by the insurance company and that claims will be met swiftly. It is particularly important that the insurers are represented by agents in all parts of the world for handling claims.

The most widely used marine cover is provided through the terms of the Institute Cargo Clauses (IC Clauses) – a schedule of clauses introduced by Lloyds of London and the Institute of London Underwriters. When and how these clauses are applied will be explained in a later chapter when insurance documents are analysed in detail.

Banks

The importance of the role played by banks in trade finance cannot be over-stressed. They provide a multitude of services to every operator in the trade chain and for every stage of any transaction. Banking instruments and techniques which have been developed over hundreds of years are made available with world-wide branch networks, affiliates and correspondents. The rapid growth of world markets owes much to the ability of these financial institutions to adapt to change, to keep pace with development and to maintain a high level of skill in handling transactions.

The most complex deals can require pre-shipment and post-shipment finance, advances against goods in transit, in warehouse, in customs or even in the consignee's possession. Apart from granting pure trade-related credit, banks protect their customers, whether exporters or importers, against every type of risk they are likely to encounter by employing a range of guarantees, standby credits and indemnities. Particular mention must be made of the importance of documentary credits and the skill that bank operators display when issuing and confirming credits, paying and negotiating documents. Exporters are able to enjoy the guarantee of payment which banks provide and importers can be confident that the documentation they have demanded has been carefully scrutinized.

In addition to finance, banks provide a number of support services essential to exporters and importers wishing to enter new markets. Credit and status reports on foreign operators, advance details of overseas contracts and government tenders are regularly supplied to customers seeking trading opportunities.

Irrespective of where they are established, all banks become involved at some time in trade finance even if only to transfer funds in settlement of a deal or to handle a simple inward documentary collection. The large international banks have vigorously followed the development of world markets and are widely represented by branches and agencies. They enjoy a huge advantage over smaller banks in their ability to provide complete financial packages for multinational transactions and to contain the whole operation within their own network. The cost-saving achieved means that they can quote very competitively and customers appreciate the confidentiality of confining their operations to one bank.

Access to a large range of currencies, particularly Eurodollars, facilitates funding for international banks and often reduces the need to go into the market for cover. A presence in any country provides up-to-date knowledge of local regulations, import and export quotas and embargoes, and opportunities to obtain information on imminent government and private contracts for which foreign tenders are invited. If needed, they can provide bonding facilities for overseas branch customers. Branches in any bank network are far more likely to attract inward collections and export documentary credits which, because of their status, they can handle without the intervention of an outside avalising or confirming bank.

The demands of world trade have led to the development of specialist banks engaged solely in the provision of all the facilities necessary for importing and exporting. These banks attract trade operators by the attention they pay to particular markets and to the economic, political and financial trends in the countries with whom they deal. For them, specialization is synonymous with skill, with the added bonus that they often enjoy financial participation from their governments.

Factors

Although factors were once in fierce competition with banks, particularly in the financing of receivables, the banks quickly realised that there was a niche for factoring in their own organization and the major banks took over a number of the leading operators. Now, most international banks have a factoring subsidiary. There is a clearly defined difference between the services offered by banks and factors.

The most important difference is the question of **recourse**. Every form of banking finance is effected **with recourse** to its customer, whereas factors provide facilities for buying debts **without recourse**. Once they accept responsibility for making a collection they assume any resultant losses. They go further in the service to exporters by carrying out the necessary bookkeeping and accounts on their behalf.

The strongest area of the factoring service lies in credit investigation, which is so accurate that they are able to assume greater risks than banks. Complete export factoring involves the exporter in handing all his documents to the factor who takes an assignment over the debt of the overseas buyer. The reader will understand that the factor considers the buyer as his debtor, the exporter having sold the debt without recourse.

Although expensive, factoring can take over a number of administrative operations for the exporter leaving him to concentrate on his main business of selling. Even for sales on open account, factors buy the receivables without recourse, assuming responsibility for the commercial, political and exchange risks.

Government agencies and international financial institutions

In times of recession and following natural disasters those countries most affected are often unable to purchase essential commodities, foodstuff and fuels. To provide assistance a number of organizations have been set up with funds subscribed by member countries. A typical example is the International Monetary Fund (IMF) which has a membership approaching

200 and provides not only aid, but research into the underlying problems in countries applying for it. Although assistance is rarely refused, the Fund imposes conditions intended to promote economic recovery. Grants to successful applicants result in traditional trade operations employing documentary credits and guarantees supported by special reimbursement arrangement.

Chapter 2

Cross-border trading

The risks involved

If there were no risks involved in international trade, sellers would transport their goods across the world by whatever means without hindrance and buyers would remit funds in payment free from any intervention by central banks and the operations of exchange control. But no transaction can be undertaken without risk to the buyer and seller, although those risks can be significantly reduced by banks and insurers.

For the **exporter** the main risks are:

- **Commercial:** delayed payment or non-payment.
- **Political:** intervention by central bank in importer's country to delay or prevent the release of foreign exchange.
- **Exchange:** depreciation in the currency in which he has invoiced his goods.

For the **importer** the main risks are:

- **Commercial:** short- or non-delivery and delivery of sub-standard goods.
- **Political:** the imposition of an export embargo in the seller's country, or an import embargo in the buyer's own country.
- **Exchange:** appreciation in the currency in which he is buying his goods.

In addition, there is always the risk to the importer that his foreign supplier will fail to produce correct documents, resulting in the customs authorities refusing entry of the goods. Unless he knows his supplier well, the only guarantee available to ensure accurate documentation is the irrevocable credit, where a bank checks all documents before accepting them from an exporter.

Although the above risks are present in any foreign trade transaction it is essential to understand what ultimate affect they will have on each party. For the exporter, **non-payment** needs little explanation and much depends on the value of the contract in question; a large contract may involve high manufacturing and transport costs and if the buyer defaults the loss can seriously jeopardize the exporter's financial situation. If that weakness becomes known in commercial circles, it can result in other buyers adopting aggressive attitudes on pricing and perhaps demanding credit.

Late payment, although less serious, still puts pressure on the exporter's finances and increases the cost of bank finance. If the exporter had anticipated payment by selling the foreign exchange forward, he would be obliged to close out the deal with a possible loss if the currency had depreciated.

Intervention by the importer's central bank in preventing the release of foreign exchange to meet a foreign supplier's invoice leaves that supplier not knowing when or if he will be paid, despite the fact that the buyer has paid in local currency. In addition to the financial damage to the supplier, there is the consideration he must give to continuing to manufacture and ship goods to the importer who has not actually breached the contract. Specifically manufactured items intended and trademarked solely for a particular importer may have to be removed from the production line.

In most cases, **non-delivery** is the worst risk faced by the importer and one which he will be concerned to cover if possible by using a banking technique. It has to be understood that goods imported into a country are going to be re-sold in the domestic market, processed and re-sold to an overseas market, or are raw materials to be consumed in a manufacturing process. Whatever they are, the goods are the subject of one or more contracts and their non-arrival almost certainly means that the importer will have to obtain alternative supplies from another source. But at what price? The cost of substitute goods may eliminate any profit the importer hoped to make. At a later stage in this book, performance guarantees will be explained and their use in protecting against non-delivery demonstrated. Importers and exporters are both vulnerable to the imposition of trade embargoes and non-renewal of import licences which prevent the completion of their contract.

Depreciation in the currency in which he has contracted to sell his goods presents the exporter with a potential loss. Conversely, the importer does not wish to see the currency **appreciate**. By using forward exchange contracts or currency options both parties can fix the rate at which settlement will eventually be made. For example, a UK exporter selling goods in January valued at US$150 000 for delivery in August would receive £100 000 if the January rate of US$1.50 : £1.00 remained constant until August. But if the dollar depreciated to US$1.75 : £1.00 he would receive only £85 714, an exchange loss of 15%. However, by selling the currency forward for delivery in August, the exporter could at least limit any adverse movement in the exchange rate. Banks buy and sell currencies for forward delivery up to and beyond 12 months. So in this case, the exporter, by selling forward in January, would know exactly what amount of sterling he would receive in August. The purpose of forward contracts is to enable operators to fix their prices for future dates, not to profit from exchange movements. Fluctuations in exchange rates can provide losses or profits, but the sensible traders use the bank facilities in order to correctly assess their liabilities or the value of their receivables.

By providing facilities for international trade finance, banks assume a wide range of risks, many of them lifted from the shoulders of their customers. Non-payment, late payment, non-delivery and political risks are generally accepted by banks in the normal course of business and much depends on their assessment of those risks if they are to avoid losses. A bigger risk for banks lies in the possibility that they may make a technical error in handling documents or in operating some of their sophisticated instruments.

Contracts

Buyers and sellers entering a market for the first time need to establish a sales contract between them. The type of contract ranges from the very simplest form of offer and acceptance to the comprehensive document required to cover the sale of high-specification technical equipment. Apart from the basic details relating to price, quantity and delivery time, there are important factors which have to be included if the separate responsibilities of the parties are to be established. Terms of sale, method of settlement, documentation and insurance must be clearly defined and understood by buyer and seller. A knowledge of **International Chamber of Commerce (ICC) Incoterms** which are set out in Table 2.1 will enable the buyer and seller to know what transport costs they are liable for and whether shipment is effected Free on Board (FOB), Cost and Freight (CFR) or Cost Insurance and Freight (CIF). The most important clause in the contract is the method of settlement, which must be agreed at the outset.

An exporter wants the most secure form of settlement to ensure that the buyer cannot take delivery of the goods before he has made payment. The importer will be equally concerned to prevent the exporter from being paid before he has delivered the goods. A number of methods of settlement are available through banks, each providing varying degrees of security for exporter and importer.

Before examining methods of settlement, it is necessary to describe the document which is present in almost every one.

The bill of exchange

It is very important that the reader fully understands the unique nature of this instrument, how it works and the role it plays in international trade. As a simple example, the cheque that anyone issues on a bank account is a bill of exchange and fulfils all the requirements of the Bills of Exchange Act 1882. In use throughout the world for over 500 years the reliability of the bill of exchange is demonstrated by the fact that the 1882 Act has hardly been amended in over 120 years. As a means of settlement and proof of payment or non-payment in legal actions, the bill of exchange has no equal.

To conform with the 1882 Act, a bill must meet certain criteria: it should be drawn by one person (drawer) in writing, addressed to another person (drawee) and signed by the drawer engaging to pay on demand or at a fixed or future date a certain sum to a named payee or to order or to bearer. In the specimens (Figs 2.1 and 2.2), the drawer is Seddon & Co, the drawee is Armstrong Baer Inc and the payee is Lloyds Bank.

Table 2.1   Summary of ICC Incoterms 2000

Methods of despatch	*Costs to be borne by:*
EXW, ex works	Buyer pays all costs from factory to final destination
FCA, free carrier	Buyer pays all costs from point of delivery
FAS, free alongside ship	Buyer pays loading charges on to vessel/sea freight/insurance
FOB, free on board	Buyer pays all costs after goods have been delivered over shipsrail
CFR, cost and freight	Seller pays all costs up to port of destination Buyer pays insurance
DEQ, delivered ex-quay	Seller pays all costs up to discharge on to quay at port of destination
DDU, delivered duty unpaid	Seller pays all costs excluding duty and taxes up to point of delivery in importing country
DDP, delivered duty paid	Seller pays all costs including duty and taxes up to point of delivery in importing country
CIF, cost insurance and freight	Seller pays all costs up to final destination
CPT, carriage paid to seller	Seller pays freight to named destination – buyer pays insurance
CIP, carriage and insurance	Seller pays freight to named destination and provides cargo insurance
DAF, delivered at frontier	Seller pays all costs to point of delivery at frontier
DES, delivered ex-ship	Seller pays all expenses up to point of unloading at port of destination

Exchange for £50,000   1ST JUNE 2003

At sight pay this FIRST of Exchange, (Second of the same tenor and date

unpaid) to the order of LLOYDS BANK PLC.

THE SUM OF FIFTY THOUSAND POUNDS

Value Received 135,000 mtrs Gingham Fabric covering contract Number

PK0-100 shipped per "YUKIKAZE" VOY: 37

To ARMSTRONG BAER INC
LENNOX PARADE
HOUSTON, USA   SEDDON & CO
                                                      THE BULLRING
                                                      BIRMINGHAM, UK

Figure 2.1

Accepted payable 30/8/2003 at Barclays Bank, Foreign Branch,
Birmingham for Armstrong Baer Inc

Exchange for £50,000   1ST JUNE 2003

At 90 DAYS pay this FIRST of Exchange, (Second of the same tenor and date

unpaid) to the order of LLOYDS BANK PLC.

THE SUM OF FIFTY THOUSAND POUNDS

Value Received 135,000 mtrs Gingham Fabric covering contract Number

PK0-100 shipped per "YUKIKAZE" VOY: 37

To ARMSTRONG BAER INC
LENNOX PARADE
HOUSTON, USA   SEDDON & CO
                                                      THE BULLRING
                                                      BIRMINGHAM, UK

Figure 2.2

At this point it is useful to interpret the main terms used to describe the operation of a bill.

- **Acceptance:** means acceptance completed by delivery.
- **Bearer:** the person in possession of a bill or note which is payable to bearer.
- **Bill:** means bill of exchange.
- **Note:** means promissory note.
- **Delivery:** transfer of possession, actual or constructive, from one person to another.
- **Holder:** the payee or endorsee of a bill or note who is in possession of it, or is the bearer thereof.
- **Endorsement:** endorsement completed by delivery.
- **Person:** includes a body of persons whether incorporated or not.
- **Value:** valuable consideration.
- **Written:** includes printed and writing including print.

The life cycle of the specimen bill would follow a fixed pattern. Once issued by Seddon it would be sent to the payee, Lloyds Bank, Birmingham who would arrange presentation to Armstrong Baer for payment and transfer of £50 000 to wherever Lloyds Bank stipulated. This bill is payable at sight but if it was a term bill, payable say 90 days after sight, it would be necessary for it to be **accepted** upon presentation. Once it has been accepted the bill becomes fully negotiable and the payee, Lloyds Bank, would be entitled to transfer it to a third party by endorsement.

Any holder unwilling to retain an accepted term bill until maturity can offer it for discount to a bank or other financial institution. Provided the bill is drawn on a sound and reliable drawee, the discounter will calculate interest for the days remaining until maturity and deduct that interest from the face value of the bill. Banks regularly rediscount such bills in the market when interest rates are favourable to them. Bills may be issued with maturities as long as 10 years or more and form the basis for forfaiting and countertrade deals.

The promissory note

A negotiable instrument, but unlike a bill of exchange it has only two parties, the drawer (promisor) and the payee (promisee – see Fig. 2.3).

LONDON 1ST JANUARY 2003

£275,000

On 31st March 2003 we promise to pay Coca Cola Limited or order at their offices in Dublin Eire the sum of Two Hundred and Seventy Five Thousand Pounds.

FOR AND ON BEHALF OF
FIZZY DRINK DISTRIBUTORS LIMITED

Figure 2.3 Promissory note

Methods of payment

Five basic methods of payment are available for settlement of international trade. They are:

1 Payment in advance.
2 Open account.
3 Bills for collection.
4 Documentary credits.
5 Standby credits

Payment in advance

Advance payment simply means that the buyer pays in advance and risks losing his money if the supplier he has paid fails to ship the goods.

Open account

Open account is a reversal of the above situation; the seller risks losing his goods by sending them direct to the buyer and allowing him to make payment in due course. Neither of these methods really involve banking facilities but it is shown in a later chapter that it is possible to protect buyer and seller from default by using banking instruments.

Bills for collection

This is a relatively inexpensive method of settlement which is very widely used. At this stage it is sufficient to provide an overview of the process; a detailed analysis and the influence of ICC rules appear in a later chapter. Briefly, immediately an exporter despatches his goods and collects the necessary shipping documents, he draws a bill of exchange on his buyer and hands it, together with the remaining documents, to his bank. His instructions to that bank will contain a request for them to forward all the documents to their correspondent in the buyer's country and for that correspondent to present them to the buyer for payment. If payment is to be made upon presentation, the bill is drawn payable at sight and the collection is known as Documents against Payment (D/P). Where the seller is granting the buyer credit, the bill will be drawn payable at a future date and the buyer can obtain the shipping documents simply by putting his acceptance on the face of the bill. In that case the collection is known as Documents against Acceptance (D/A).

Neither D/P nor D/A collections are without risk to buyer and seller; a later chapter will assess those risks and consider possible action to reduce or eliminate them.

Documentary credits

This is undoubtedly the most secure method of payment available to exporters and also provides a high degree of protection for importers. Developed by the banking industry over the past 200 years, it owes its prominence firstly to its flexibility and secondly to the skills of banking operatives who have adapted it for use in every conceivable area of trade finance. The actual credit is an undertaking addressed by a bank (the issuing bank) to a beneficiary (the exporter) on the instructions of the applicant (the importer). It undertakes that the beneficiary will be paid up to the amount detailed, provided that he presents the required documents within the validity of the credit and to whichever bank the issuing bank nominates as its agent. That, perhaps, is an oversimplification, because documentary credits can be rather complicated when structured to meet particular transactions. It is a guarantee of payment, but a **conditional** one. Despite the many years that the documentary credit has been in use, it is only in the past 40 years that a true international code of practice has been introduced to provide guidance for operating banks. The International Chamber of Commerce (ICC) produced its Uniform Customs & Practice for

Documentary Credits (UCP) in 1933. In 1962 its use became official and banks began adopting it across the world.

The code was originally drawn up from the study of documentary credits practice worldwide and was intended to unify procedures developed by international banks. Amended in 1974, 1983, 1993, and 2007 UCP600 the publication has benefited from decisions in a variety of legal actions involving documentary credits. The rules are not law but simply guidelines for all parties involved in trade finance. Strict compliance with UCP600 by any litigant will almost certainly influence the findings of a commercial court.

UCP600 will be discussed at length in a later chapter, although at this stage it is important to understand how it is structured and what factors have influenced its development. The rules deal in sequence with the life of credits from issue and the responsibilities of the banks involved, through to the handling of documents, negotiation, reimbursement, transfer and assignment. Considerable effort has been made in five issues of UCP to differentiate between the numerous transport documents being brought into use. There were criticisms of UCP500, especially in the way it attempted to rectify certain weaknesses in UCP400. The rules are intended to unify world-wide practices and in UCP 600, I CC have at last grasped the nettle (partly!) and have recognized the difficulties banks face when negotiating documents against credits issued by banks with whom they have no relationship and who present obvious political risks. Banks, shippers, carriers, forwarders and insurers are between them expected to smooth the flow of international trade and banks particularly should be allowed to assess risk and act accordingly while at the same time making every endeavour to assist completion of international transactions. From time to time ICC publishes its decisions on cases submitted to them or makes constructive comment if it is unable to find solutions within UCP600. These publications are useful reading for students of trade finance and highlight the difficulties which often confront banks in their attempts to keep within the rules.

Standby credits

This is a relatively new instrument, devised in the United States as a means of countering laws which forbid US and Japanese banks to issue on-demand guarantees. It is known as a negative credit because it is generally payable when the applicant fails to meet his commitments to the beneficiary. The beneficiary simply claims against the standby credit by presenting a statement to the effect that a certain event has not taken place (for example, an invoice submitted to the applicant has not been paid on time).

The standby is particularly useful to cover shipments of oil where the Bills of Lading are not available.

Additional methods of payment

In addition to the traditional methods of payment there are three special techniques which should be noted at this point.

Forfaiting: a facility for financing medium- and long-term contracts for exports of capital equipment. The process revolves around a specialist market prepared to buy and sell bills of exchange and promissory notes drawn on foreign importers and bearing the guarantees of their central banks. Exporters are able to finance their sales by non-recourse discounting of those instruments through forfaiting companies.

Countertrade: the creation of deals between importers in countries with little or no foreign exchange to pay for imports and exporters prepared to supply them with essential goods. Payment to the exporters can be in several forms, part goods or services, part foreign exchange and part in switch currency. The deals may involve the movement of goods between a number of different countries before the original exporter is paid. Both forfaiting and countertrade deals use all the accepted short-term methods of payment in their overall structure, as will be demonstrated in a later chapter.

Purchase of receivables provides a means for exporters to raise cash on debts due or becoming due to them from overseas buyers. It is a simple process by which a bank purchases the debts and is repaid by direct settlement from the buyers. The principal factors which may persuade an exporter to enter into this form of finance are firstly the rate of interest he is paying on his overdraft, secondly the time taken by his buyers to settle their accounts, and finally the need to purchase assets with a higher yield. The fact that the exporter is selling on open account suggests that the buyers are a good credit risk, although the bank must verify that. If it agrees to provide a facility, the bank sets limits on each buyer up to which it will purchase receivables on them, estimated for a period of, say, one month. The bank then advances the equivalent of the debts and credits the exporter with the proceeds. Payment by the buyers is made direct to the bank who may or may not accept the risks of non-payment and default without recourse to the exporter.

Chapter 3

Bills for collection

When there is a level of trust between buyer and seller, the seller may be prepared to agree to a method of payment which is considerably less expensive than documentary credits. The method is entitled **bill for collection** and is used throughout the world, probably accounting for the majority of all foreign settlements. It is fundamentally simple in operation and allows the exporter to ship his goods, obtain a bill of lading and collect payment by way of a bill of exchange through the use of his own bank and a bank in the importer's country.

Parties to a collection

- Exporter (drawer)
- Remitting bank
- Collecting bank
- Importer (drawee)
- Avalising bank (exceptionally)

There are two types of bills for collection, D/P and D/A. Those terms determine what the importer is required to do in order to obtain release of the documents and take delivery of the goods.

D/P bill for collection (documents against payment)

This is a **sight** collection where the bill of exchange is drawn payable upon presentation to the drawee. Upon payment, the documents of title to the

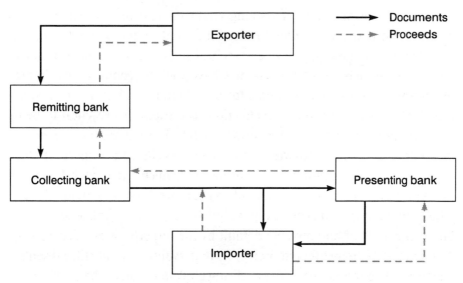

Figure 3.1   D/P documentary collection

goods are released. To achieve this, a series of operations must be carried out by the exporter, his bank (the **remitting bank**) and an overseas agent selected by the remitting bank (the **collecting bank**).

The exporter draws his bill of exchange and delivers it, complete with a set of shipping documents to the remitting bank (see Fig. 3.1). A typical set of documents will comprise invoice, certificate of origin, bill of lading and a certificate of insurance (for CIF shipments). The exporter's instructions to that bank must take account of possible eventualities which can threaten the security of his shipment. These additional instructions are intended to guide the collecting bank in dealing with the exporter's goods if the importer refuses to pay.

D/A bill for collection (documents against acceptance)

It is normal in international trade for the buyer to request credit from the seller. He may wish to make payment at a future date after he has taken delivery of the goods. If the seller agrees, the bill of exchange accompanying the collection is drawn payable, say, 30, 60 or 90 days after sight.

The reasons for an importer seeking credit depend on the nature of his business. He may require time to resell the goods, often on credit; he may have to split the consignment when received and re-pack it for distribution to a variety of outlets. As a trader he may have sold the goods on to a foreign buyer and requires the documents for presentation against a documentary credit or even under a further collection. The exporter's reaction to being asked for credit is reflected in the terms which he instructs his bank to include in the collection. If the exporter does not wish to allow the importer to take delivery of the goods simply by accepting a bill which might be dishonoured at maturity, he can ask for a local bank to guarantee its payment. In this case, a bank in the importing country, possibly the importer's bank, endorses the bill '*bon pour aval*' and possible default by the importer is avoided (see Fig. 3.2). It must be remembered, however, that avalising a bill still presents a political risk to the exporter. The avalising bank may fail, or the central bank may block the release of the foreign exchange.

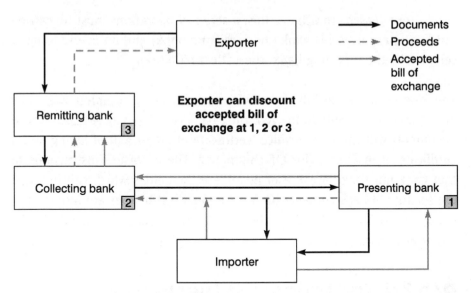

Figure 3.2 D/A documentary collection

A typical collection for goods despatched by sea will comprise:

- bill of exchange
- invoice
- certificate of origin

- insurance certificate or policy
- transport document

The documents must all be properly endorsed, where necessary, to enable the collecting bank to give the importer a good title to the goods on release.

Drawer	
Consignee	Drawee (if not Consignee)
To Bank	

FORWARD DOCUMENTS ENUMERATED BELOW BY AIRMAIL FOLLOW SPECIAL INSTRUCTIONS AND THOSE MARKED X							
Bill of exchange	Invoice	Cert/Invoice	Cert Origin	Insurance Pol/Cert	B/Lading	Parcel Post Receipt	Airway Bill
Combined Transport Doc	Other Documents						

Release Documents on	Acceptance	Payment	If unaccepted		Protest/Do not protest
If documents not taken up on arrival of goods	Warehouse goods/ Do not warehouse goods		and advise reason by		Telex/Airmail
	Insure/Do not insure		If unpaid		Protest/Do not protest
Collect all Charges			and advise reason by		Telex/Airmail
Collect Correspondent Charges Only			Advise acceptance and due date by		Telex/Airmail
Return Accepted Bill by Airmail			Return Proceeds by		Telex/Airmail
In case of need refer to			For guidance		Accept their instructions
Special Instructions					

Figure 3.3 Specimen collection letter

These are details which a remitting bank is not obliged to check unless it is financing the collection, when it will ensure that the documents are endorsed to its order. Instructions to the exporter's bank for handling the collection will be contained in a special form provided by the banks in line with the specimen shown in Figure 3.3.

The **remitting bank** now takes charge of the collection and ensures that the exporter's instructions are carefully observed in accordance with Uniform Rules for Collections (522). Although not obliged to examine the documents, apart from ascertaining that it has a complete set, the remitting bank makes sure that the bill of exchange, bill of lading and insurance document (if any) are properly drawn up and endorsed in such a manner as to enable the collecting bank to pass a good title to the buyer. When the remitting bank has a financial interest in the collection it obviously takes great care to protect its title to the goods by having the bill of exchange and bill of lading endorsed to its order by the exporter. A collection instruction is prepared by the bank addressed to its agent in the buyer's country, the collecting bank. The collection instruction contains a number of actions which the collecting bank is asked to carry out in obtaining settlement of the collection. The specimen of a remitting bank's schedule shown here sets out those requirements clearly. Of greatest importance are the instructions to be followed in the event of non-payment or non-acceptance of the bill of exchange.

The responsibilities of remitting and collecting banks are set out in the ICC Rules (Publication No. 522) and come into force immediately a remitting bank accepts documents for collection.

The **collecting bank**, on receipt of a D/P collection, first checks to ensure that it has the complete set; it does not check the individual documents. The drawee is contacted and requested to pay the bill of exchange and take up the documents; once payment is made, the bank will transfer the funds back to the remitting bank. This is an appropriate time to mention two important conditions to be observed by the collecting bank. In accordance with Uniform Rules for Collections it must advise the remitting bank immediately of payment or non-payment/non-acceptance. In the case of payment, this enables the exporter to:

1 Sell the foreign currency.
2 Despatch further goods in the knowledge that his buyer appears to be a reliable payer.
3 Release bank facilities for financing further transactions.

In the event of non-payment or non-acceptance, this enables the exporter to:

1 Decide what to do with his goods which may have arrived or are about to arrive at a foreign port. He may already have included guidance for this eventuality in his instruction to the remitting bank.
2 To withhold further shipments to the buyer concerned until the reasons for default are made clear.
3 To notify his export credit insurers (if any).

The security offered to an exporter using D/P collection is limited to protecting his goods if the collection is unpaid. This is sometimes of little comfort to him if the goods are in a foreign port where they may be liable to theft and damage or seizure.

D/A collections are handled in the same way as D/P collections except that the collecting bank is authorized to release the documents immediately the importer accepts the term bill of exchange. This is the point at which the exporter assumes the risk that, having accepted a bill and taken delivery of the goods, the importer will fail to honour the bill at maturity. For that reason, exporters do not lightly agree to D/A collections and require first-class reports on the importer before doing so and even then try to limit the period of credit; 30 to 60 days is quite common and periods beyond that indicate the higher credit rating of the importer. Advice of acceptance and the maturity date is sent without delay to the remitting bank. In normal circumstances the bill is held by the collecting bank until maturity but, exceptionally, it may be requested to discount it and remit the net proceeds to the remitting bank. A number of factors govern discounting, which will be explained at the end of this chapter.

The possibility that a drawee will refuse to honour a sight bill or accept a term bill is always present and when it happens the collecting bank can be involved in a considerable amount of work. Non-payment triggers a number of actions on the part of the collecting bank depending on the instructions received from the remitting bank. The unpaid exporter wishes to protect his goods which, when they arrive at the port of destination, have to be cleared from the carrying vessel. The carrier will not release the goods if freight has not yet been paid (FOB shipment); once released they have to be securely warehoused and insured. There is no duty upon the collecting bank to comply with these instructions and it only does so if it is satisfied that the remitting bank will reimburse the various charges, which can be considerable. This is a good point at which to remind the reader of the importance to the remitting bank of selecting a reliable agent to act as collecting bank; international banks have an enormous advantage in these situations when they are employing their own branches or affiliates.

Warehousing should be effected with an operator known to the collecting bank as reliable and trustworthy. The goods are often insured with a local company or by the exporter immediately he is advised of non-payment. The value of using a bill of exchange is shown when for non-payment the collecting bank can, if instructed, have it noted and protested. This is a legal process carried out by a local public notary or an authorized solicitor, who re-presents the bill to the drawee and if he still refuses to honour it, places his certification of non-payment on the bill. Noting and protesting are essential if a bill is to be sued on and provides acceptable proof of non-payment.

Quite often an importer tries to delay payment as long as he can, and if the carrying vessel is not scheduled to arrive for a week or two he may even assure the collecting bank that he will pay or accept the bill when it does. Generally, the collecting bank is not authorized to allow this and advises the remitting bank of non-payment or non-acceptance and passes on the drawee's statement of intention to pay or accept on arrival of the carrying vessel.

Non-acceptance of a bill requires the same swift action by a collecting bank, although the drawee's refusal may not be as final as if the bill were drawn payable at sight.

The actions required to be taken by the collecting bank in the event of non-payment or non-acceptance of a collection are generally set out in the remitting bank's instructions. At the same time, the bank must comply with the appropriate articles of Uniform Rules for Collections. So far as the exporter is concerned, the situation may be serious, depending on the value of the collection. He is in the unenviable position of having his goods stored in a foreign warehouse, incurring a variety of local costs and will have to pay the freight if shipment is effected FOB. The reason for non-payment or non-acceptance will influence further trade with the buyer: is he in financial difficulties? Are the goods unacceptable? Has he simply exceeded his bank's facilities for financing his imports?

Each scenario presents the exporter with a different problem requiring appropriate action. If the buyer is temporarily in financial difficulties but has hitherto been a very prompt payer, it may be wise to allow him time to pay (and if so, how long?). Unacceptable goods can possibly be modified locally at a cost less than that which re-shipping them to a new buyer might incur; alternatively, the exporter can offer the buyer a discount. As a last resort, if all other remedies fail, the exporter must seek another buyer, preferably local. Where possible, an exporter is asked by the remitting bank if he can provide them with the name of an associate company or friendly correspondent in the importer's country or town of residence, prepared to assist in negotiating with buyers when collections are refused. This appointee is known as a '**case of need**' whose level of authority to undertake certain formalities on behalf of the exporter must be advised to the collecting bank. In certain circumstances, the case of need may be authorized to take delivery of the goods, insure and warehouse them and endeavour to find another buyer. The collecting bank must ascertain the level of authority before accepting any instructions from the case of need.

Banks cannot be expected to become involved in disputes between buyers and sellers. The exporter himself may be placed in a difficult situation following non-payment of a substantial collection, particularly if it has been financed by his bank. Repayment of any advance can be demanded and the bank may remove the importer's name from its facilities. At this point, the question arises as to whether the exporter has export credit insurance which covers non-payment or refusal of the goods by the importer. If he has, he may have a valid claim but must usually wait some months before settlement. Normally, when banks finance collections, they take an assignment of the export credit policy as additional security.

The collection processes discussed so far have involved the use of remitting banks, but in exceptional circumstances exporters' banks allow their customers to send their collections direct to an approved correspondent with instructions that all proceeds are remitted back direct to their bank. This procedure may well suit the exporter's bank, particularly if the collection documentation is heavy; banks do not, as a rule, take on pure collection work unless there are side benefits. The method is cheaper for the exporter, whose instructions to the collection bank are on special forms provided by his own bank so he can be sure the service provided will be fully in accordance with those instructions and with Uniform Rules for Collection. Banks are prepared even to finance these direct collections, provided they receive the proceeds direct and despite the fact that, in this instance, they may have no title to the goods through the documents of despatch.

Uniform Rules for Collections (Publication No. 522)

Article 2. Definition of a collection

The handling by banks of documents in accordance with instructions received in order to:

(a) Obtain payment or acceptance; or
(b) Deliver documents against payment and/or acceptance; or
(c) Deliver documents on other terms and conditions.

'Documents' means:
(i)   Financial documents: bills of exchange, promissory notes, cheques or other similar instruments used for obtaining the payment of money.
(ii) Commercial documents: invoices, transport documents, documents of title or other similar documents or any other documents whatsoever, not being financial documents.

A **clean collection** is any collection of financial documents **not accompanied by commercial documents**.

Article 6

For documents payable at sight the presenting bank must make presentation for **payment without delay**.

For documents payable at a tenor, where acceptance is called for, the presenting bank must make presentation for **acceptance without delay**.

Article 9

Banks will act in good faith and exercise reasonable care.

Article 10 (d)

Any charges and/or expenses incurred by banks in connection with any action taken to protect the goods will be for account of the party from whom they were received for collection.

Article 10 (e)(ii)

Where a collecting bank on the instructions of the remitting bank arranges for the release of the goods, the remitting bank shall indemnify such collecting bank for all damages and expenses incurred.

Article 12

Banks must immediately inform the party from whom a collection is received if any document is missing or is found not to be as listed.

Article 16

Amounts collected must be made available without delay to the party from whom the collection was received.

Articles 20 and 21

Where bank charges and interest are to be collected from the drawee (importer) but are not paid, the collecting bank may not waive them unless specifically authorized to do so. Where no authority to waive is given, the collecting bank must not deliver the documents to the drawee.

Article 24

The collection instruction should give specific instructions regarding protest in the event of non-payment or non-acceptance.

Article 25

Collecting banks will not accept any instructions from the case of need unless they are clearly within the authority detailed in the remitting bank's instructions.

Article 26 (c)(i)

The collecting bank must send without delay advice of payment.

Article 26 (c)(ii)

The collecting bank must send without delay advice of acceptance.

Article 26 (c)(iii)

The collecting bank must send without delay advice of non-payment and/or non-acceptance.

Discounting bills of exchange is a regular service provided to trade operators by banks, factors and finance houses. Any term bill, payable at a future date, may be available for discount depending on the strength of the parties to it. If a bill has been accepted by a bank, the possibility of it being paid at maturity is clearly greater than if the drawee is an unknown individual or a small corporate entity. The payee may not wish to wait, say, 60 or 90 days before he receives his money and is prepared to pay the price for taking early payment. A bank discounting a bill of exchange will calculate interest for the number of days it has to run before maturity and will deduct it from the amount of the bill. That rate of interest will reflect the quality of the drawee; a low rate for a bank, increasing as the credit rating of the drawee decreases.

Chapter 4

The irrevocable documentary credit

As a method of payment, this instrument has no equal; it is completely flexible, versatile and accepted universally. Although it is only a **conditional guarantee**, its value to an exporter facing the risks involved in trading with a foreign country is undoubted. In essence, the documentary credit is an undertaking given by a bank (the issuing bank) on behalf of its customer (the applicant) to make payment to a named exporter (the beneficiary) upon presentation of stipulated documents relating to the supply of goods or services. It must have a fixed validity, generally not exceeding 12 months, must show with which bank it is available and must be for an amount payable in currency.

So far as the exporter is concerned, the main benefit to him of an irrevocable credit lies in the fact that it provides him with an undertaking to make settlement **given by a bank**. He is thus relieved of any concern he may have over the ability or willingness of the importer to pay him. In addition, he knows that once issued, an irrevocable credit cannot be cancelled or amended without his agreement.

The importer who, as applicant, controls much of the terminology and documentation of a credit knows that it will protect him against any attempt by his supplier to obtain payment before his goods have actually been despatched. In addition he can be certain that the documents presented under the credit will be carefully scrutinized by the negotiating bank and the issuing bank, thus avoiding any difficulties in clearing the goods through customs.

Parties to a documentary credit

Applicant: the importer (buyer) who submits an application for the opening of a credit and who stipulates its terms and documentary requirements.

Issuing bank: the bank which prepares the credit in accordance with the applicant's instructions and issues it addressed to the beneficiary.

Advising/nominated bank: the bank selected by the issuing bank to authenticate the credit and advise it to the beneficiary.

Confirming bank: any bank which adds its confirmation to a credit.

Beneficiary: the exporter (seller) to whom the credit is addressed and to whom the issuing bank gives its irrevocable undertaking.

Negotiating bank: generally speaking it is the nominated or confirming bank which negotiates documents presented to it against a credit which it has advised. By negotiating the bank advances the value of the documents to the beneficiary and reimburses itself in accordance with the issuing bank's instructions. If a delay in obtaining reimbursement is anticipated, the negotiating bank may charge interest on the advance payment. It is not uncommon for documentary credits to be **freely negotiable**, that is any bank may negotiate documents and avail itself of the reimbursement arrangements. Whether the negotiating bank is the nominated bank or any bank negotiating a freely negotiable credit, if it has not confirmed the credit, it negotiates as agent of the beneficiary and not as agent of the issuing bank. Consequently, it has recourse to the beneficiary should it fail to obtain reimbursement from the issuing bank. Negotiating banks take risks when handling documents under other bank's credits and there are a number of legal cases which demonstrate the difficulties in which they may find themselves. A detailed assessment of those risks and the application of UCP600 is given in a later chapter.

Reimbursing bank: an agent appointed by the issuing bank with authority to reimburse a bank which has effected a negotiation or made a payment against a credit established by the issuing bank.

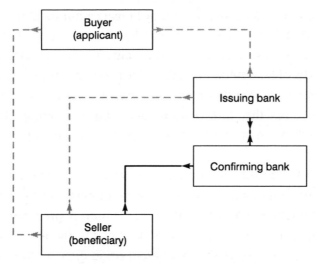

Figure 4.1 Contractual relationship between parties to a confirmed irrevocable credit

The complete life cycle of a documentary credit from issue to final settlement involves the above parties and a number of contracts are created as shown in Figure 4.1.

Irrevocable documentary credits are divided into three basic categories:

1 **Sight**. The sight credit enables the beneficiary to be paid immediately upon presentation of documents which comply with its terms. However, it may be available either with a bank in the beneficiary's country or with the issuing bank. Obviously, the beneficiary prefers payment locally; firstly because of the time factor and secondly because a local bank can assist him in obtaining payment from the issuing bank if his documents are found to be out of order.

   Although sight credits may call for a bill of exchange, it is often waived if not presented. The significance of the sight bill of exchange will be discussed in a later chapter relating to negotiation.

2 **Usance**. Available by the acceptance of a bill of exchange drawn by the beneficiary and payable at a fixed or determinable future date. Acceptance is made by the negotiating or issuing bank when documents are presented in order and the accepted bill is handed back to the

beneficiary. As a term bill, it cannot be paid until its maturity date but the fact that it has been accepted by a bank means that it can be discounted by the beneficiary for cash. Usance credits enable the importer to obtain credit, generally for a maximum of 365 days, but it must be stressed here that many importers cannot obtain credit on their own standing; the intervention of a bank offering the exporter guaranteed payment will often persuade him to agree to delayed settlement.

It is not difficult to imagine the situation where an exporter is considering entering into a contract with a foreign buyer and expects to be paid at sight. For a sight settlement, he may be prepared to use a D/P collection, but if the buyer then requests credit, the risk to the exporter changes immediately. Rather than grant credit direct to the buyer, he will demand a usance irrevocable credit under which he knows payment is guaranteed by a bank. That way, the exporter is secured and the importer gets his credit, although he will have to bear the issuing bank's charges.

3 **Deferred payment**. This type of credit has become increasingly used when the exporter's fiscal authorities insist that a stamp duty be paid on bills of exchange. This can be costly so the deferred payment credit has no bill of exchange but instead, upon presentation of documents which the negotiating or issuing bank considers to be in order, the beneficiary is given a **letter of undertaking** by which the bank agrees to pay on a fixed future date. The weakness of this type of credit is demonstrated by the fact that a letter of undertaking is not a negotiable instrument; it cannot be transferred by endorsement to give a good title to the endorsee. At a later point in the book the dangers of negotiating banks agreeing to discount this document will be discussed (Banco Santander SA v. Banque Paribas, Feb 2000).

Revocable

Mention should be made here of the **revocable** documentary credit which, although it was once in general use, has so declined in popularity that it is now rarely used. The reason is simple: the revocable credit can be amended or cancelled by the applicant or the issuing bank without requiring the agreement of the beneficiary. However, if the bank with whom the revocable credit is available negotiates documents prior to receipt of a notice of cancellation, the issuing bank is obliged to reimburse the negotiating bank.

The documentary credit can be issued by teletransmission or mail, both methods may follow the standard forms recommended by the International Chamber of Commerce. Any credit issued by SWIFT (Society for Worldwide Interbank Financial Telecommunications) is automatically considered to be subject to UCP600 without including a specific statement to that effect.

Constructing the credit

The applicant

Prepares instructions for his bank with the intention of ensuring that the resultant credit will meet with the exporter's requirements (as per sales contract) and at the same time provide the precise documents necessary to clear the goods on importation. He is cautioned by the issuing bank not to include excessive detail in his application and also not to make the credit too difficult for the beneficiary to use under normal conditions.

The issuing bank

Constructing the credit to comply with the applicant's instruction often requires considerable diplomacy on the part of the issuing bank. The application forms the basis of a contract between applicant and issuer and consequently misinterpretation of its customer's instructions could render the bank liable for any loss suffered by the applicant. It is always open to the issuer to revert to the applicant for clarification of any apparent ambiguity in the application. The courts will generally uphold any reasonable interpretation arrived at by the issuing bank where the application contained ambiguities (Midland Bank v. Seymour, 1955). A poorly constructed credit reflects badly on the issuing bank, may mislead a negotiating bank and certainly can put the issuer at risk. By its very nature an irrevocable credit once issued and accepted by the beneficiary constitutes a contract between those parties. A negotiation effected within the terms of such a credit would oblige the issuing bank to make reimbursement, even if it was unable to obtain payment from the applicant if the latter claims that his instructions have been incorrectly interpreted. The whole purpose of an exporter requesting to be paid by way of an irrevocable credit is so that he can be sure:

■ to be paid or have a bill accepted or to be given an undertaking of future payment **on presentation of documents**
■ to be paid in his own country (preferably in his own town)
■ to be paid in the currency of his sales contract
■ to have a local bank handling amendments, indemnities and queries.

On the other hand, the importer expects:

■ to have the credit opened exactly as instructed by him
■ to have it advised through a competent bank
■ to be assured that the beneficiary can only be paid against correct documents and within the validity of the credit.

The irrevocable credit, when prepared for despatch by the issuing bank, should contain a number of essential details:

1 That it is revocable (Article 6).
2 The name of the bank with whom it is available.
3 Name and address of beneficiary.
4 An amount in currency.
5 A fixed expiry date.
6 Term: at sight, usance or deferred payment.
7 Latest date of shipment.
8 Whether part shipments and trans-shipment are permitted.
9 Place of taking in charge or port of shipment.
10 Port of destination.
11 Documents required.
12 A description of the goods.
13 Term of despatch (as per Incoterms).
14 The period of time after the date of shipment during which the documents must be presented.

15 To be confirmed or not.

16 Reimbursement instructions.

17 Indication that it is subject to UCP600.

The finished credit should not contain any conditions which are not evidenced by specific documents. It is a **documentary** credit and therefore every obligation placed upon the beneficiary in order for him to obtain payment should be the subject of a document or documents. Furthermore, the issuing bank must discourage the applicant from inserting too much detail (Article 4) and should not allow the inclusion of any document

---

SPECIMEN

ISSUE OF A DOCUMENTARY CREDIT   **** SWIFT NORMAL ****

SENDER: *RECEIVER:*

* FORM OF DOCUMENTARY CREDIT *
* DOCUMENTARY CREDIT NUMBER *
* DATE OF ISSUE *
* DATE AND PLACE OF EXPIRY *
* APPLICANT *
* BENEFICIARY *
* CURRENCY CODE, AMOUNT *
* AVAILABLE WITH . . . . BY . . . . *
* PARTIAL SHIPMENTS *
* TRANSHIPMENT *
* LOADING ON BOARD/DESPATCH/TAKING IN CHARGE AT /FROM *
* FOR TRANSPORTATION TO . . . . *
* LATEST DATE OF SHIPMENT *
* DESCRIPTION OF GOODS AND/OR SERVICES *
* DOCUMENTS REQUIRED *
* ADDITIONAL CONDITIONS *
* CHARGES*
* CONFIRMATION INSTRUCTIONS *
* REIMBURSEMENT BANK *
* SENDER TO RECEIVER INFORMATION *
* INSTRUCTIONS TO PAYING/ACCEPTING/NEGOTIATING BANK *

Figure 4.2

requiring the countersignature of the applicant or even approval on his part before it becomes good tender under the credit. Obviously, to allow such conditions destroys the irrevocability of the credit. It is the issuing bank's credit, not the applicant's credit.

When issued, almost always by telex, the outward documentary credit will look like the specimen shown in Figure 4.2.

Issuing the credit

The advising/nominated bank

The issuing bank selects a foreign bank, or one of its own branches, to act as its agent for the purpose of authenticating the credit and advising it to the beneficiary. That bank is known as the advising or nominated bank and if it declines to advise the credit, as it is entitled to, it must immediately inform the issuing bank.

According to Article 12, in addition to advising the credit, the nominated bank may agree to undertake certain responsibilities under the credit. If the bank advises the beneficiary of its agreement to comply with Article 10c it could eventually be involved in:

■ making payment under the credit
■ accepting a bill of exchange
■ issuing a deferred payment undertaking.

However, since there is no consideration for the nominated bank giving its agreement, such agreement cannot be enforced against it. There is no contractual relationship between the nominated bank and the beneficiary.

The beneficiary must therefore be careful not to rely too heavily on any agreement given by the nominated bank. Realistically, it is only necessary to consider the position of a nominated bank which, upon advising another bank's credit, informed the beneficiary that it would be prepared, eventually, to pay, accept a bill of exchange or issue a deferred payment order. If, during the validity of the credit, the creditworthiness of the issuing bank deteriorated, the nominated bank may be obliged to withdraw its agreement and even decline to negotiate the beneficiary's documents. Similarly, a change in the quality of the political risk involved in dealing with the issuing bank's country may mean that although that bank may honour a claim from the nominated bank for a negotiation of documents, the country's central bank may fail to release the foreign currency to meet the claim.

Both of these risks, commercial and political, have already been referred to in cross-border trading and a nominated bank sensibly will not accept them unless it is contractually obliged to; in other words, only if it has confirmed the credit. It may be asked by the issuing bank to add its confirmation to the credit or if the credit provides for pre-shipment finance to make an advance to the beneficiary. Neither of these requests need be acted upon by the advising bank, but if it declines to carry them out it must advise the issuing bank without delay and simply proceed with advising and authenticating the credit. Confirming a credit, as will be shown in later chapters, involves the bank in a number of obligations and risks which it may feel it does not wish to assume.

The confirming bank

The position of the confirming bank is entirely different from that of the nominated bank. For a consideration, namely a confirmation commission, the confirming bank undertakes to pay, accept a bill of exchange or issue a deferred payment undertaking under another bank's credit. It therefore assumes responsibility for the commercial and political risks involved and enters into a contract with the beneficiary from which it cannot withdraw. This is precisely what makes the confirmed irrevocable credit the most secure method of settlement available to an exporter.

Although the confirming bank is usually the one through which the credit is advised, it is not uncommon for confirmation to be added by a third party bank; that bank may even be in a different country. A credit which is available with a bank in Brussels may be confirmed by a bank in Geneva. The reason for this arrangement is simply that the issuing bank has a confirmation facility with a Geneva bank, but no similar facility with the advising bank.

This situation can create problems when the confirming bank stipulates that its confirmation is conditional upon the relative documents being presented to it before they are despatched to the issuing bank. This is done to obtain the protection of Article 8. It is only necessary to consider the risks involved in confirming credits to understand the reasoning behind the confirming bank's condition.

The beneficiary

The beneficiary will receive advice of the credit and should study its terms in order to understand exactly what he has to do to eventually obtain payment. Any terms or conditions which he finds unacceptable must be made known to the applicant, **not the advising bank**, with a request that the credit be amended. When it fully meets with the beneficiary's requirements he can take whatever action is needed to prepare his goods for shipment.

Eventually he will present his documents either to the nominated or confirming bank for payment or acceptance, or to any bank prepared to negotiate them if the credit is stated to be freely negotiable. He can only be certain of payment or acceptance without recourse if presentation is made either to the issuing bank or the confirming bank. No other bank, nominated or otherwise, is *obliged* to negotiate.

Reimbursement

It is essential that an irrevocable documentary credit stipulates the manner in which a negotiating bank will be reimbursed; this may be effected in several ways.

1 By the debit of an account held by the issuing bank with the claiming bank.
2 The issuing bank will make reimbursement upon receipt from the claiming bank of the relative documents, in order.

3 The issuing bank will make reimbursement upon receipt of a telegraphic claim from the claiming bank.
4 The claiming bank is authorized to make a telegraphic claim for reimbursement on a specific bank appointed by the issuing bank and named in the credit.

The reimbursing bank

Where the credit allows reimbursement to be claimed from an appointed bank, the issuing bank provides it with limited details of the credit, namely credit number, amount, any tolerances, expiry date and the name of the bank entitled to claim.

No copy of the credit or any amendment thereto may be provided to the reimbursing bank, which must honour claims without the claiming bank providing a certificate of compliance with the credit terms.

In some cases the reimbursing bank is authorized to:

- accept a term draft drawn on it by the claiming bank
- issue a reimbursement undertaking addressed to the nominated or confirming bank. This undertaking is irrevocable and cannot be amended without the agreement of the bank to which it is addressed.

Uniform Rules for Bank-to-Bank Reimbursement under Documentary Credits (Publication No. 525) apply to all reimbursement authorities incorporated in the texts of documentary credits.

Documents required under documentary credits

A set of documents presented against an irrevocable credit can be said to paint a picture. They do not all describe the goods and parties in precisely the same way, but put together they should be acceptable as truly relating to the shipment to which they refer. Each document must contain an essential detail of the shipment; a packing note must list the packages, their numbers and marks and needs only to refer to their contents. Similarly, a weight note must show the gross and net weights; otherwise it is not a weight note.

In Banque de l'Indochine et de Suez v. Rayner (Mincing Lane, 1981), it was held that four certificates of origin (EUR certificates) each for 250m tons of sugar could not be positively proved to relate to the 1000m tons of sugar shipped under an irrevocable credit and described as 1000m tons in the invoice. That case was an excellent example of the fine line between an acceptable document and a non-acceptable one.

It was held in Midland Bank v. Seymour (1955) that 'every document, even if it did not contain all the particulars specified in the credit, must contain enough of the particulars to make it a valid document.'

The **invoice**, of all the documents required under a credit, is the one which must be completely accurate in certain respects. The name of the beneficiary, the description of the goods and the applicant's name must be exactly as shown in the credit advice. If a beneficiary finds that his name is misspelled in the original credit and is unable to have an amendment effected before completion of his documents, he must repeat this misspelling in his invoice if he wishes to avoid the possibility of rejection by the negotiating/paying bank. This may seem absurd, but in United Bank Ltd v. Banque Nationale de Paris and Others, the original credit advice omitted the word 'Plc' from the beneficiary's name. Although an expert witness vouched that the inclusion of 'Plc' in the documents presented was 'commercially insignificant' as an irregularity, the court upheld the bank's decision to reject the documents. That case demonstrated the difficulty facing banks having to distinguish between the application of common sense and what amounts to special knowledge.

As a general rule, the invoice should be expected to show, in addition to the names and addresses of buyer and seller and the description of goods:

- weight, quantity, unit price and total price
- shipment terms (Incoterms)
- terms of settlement
- method of transport, port of loading or place of despatch and port or place of discharge

- shipping marks
- certification or legalization when called for by the credit
- an amount which does not exceed the credit amount (unless specifically permitted by the credit terms).

The **certificate of origin** is one of the most important documents required in cross-border trading and failure to properly describe the goods or their origin can result in customs authorities refusing them entry. It is a signed statement providing evidence of the origin of the goods and is frequently required to be issued by an independent organization, which may be a chamber of commerce, and legalized by a consular representative in the exporting country.

Although Article 14 permits acceptance of a certificate of origin as tendered, if the credit simply calls for that document without further detail, an issuing or confirming bank would be well advised to question this point in the importer's application. It has to be borne in mind that until the importer reimburses the issuing bank for documents which it has paid, the relative goods belong to the bank and it would not want to run the risk of entry being refused on the grounds that the origin was in doubt. The origin of the goods can considerably influence their market price.

The **insurance certificate or policy** is rarely called for in documentary credits following gradual pressure from importing countries unwilling to use valuable foreign exchange for insurance which can be equally well effected by themselves. Where shipment is to be effected CIF, the credit stipulates the type of insurance document required and details the risks against which insurance is to be effected. The document presented must be that specified in the credit; if a policy is called for, a certificate is unacceptable. It should describe the goods in a manner not inconsistent with the other documents and should show:

- shipping marks
- vessel's name
- ports of shipment and destination
- that cover is effected at latest from date of despatch as evidenced by the transport document

- that cover is for the CIF value of the consignment plus 10%
- that it is issued in the same currency as the credit
- the name of the agent responsible for handing any claims.

Finally, it must be in a form which enables it to be transferred by endorsement.

Transport documents

To transport goods around the world by sea, air, road, rail and inland waterways involves numerous types of carriers who issue a variety of documents evidencing receipt and detailing points of despatch, destination and mode of transport. The main documents which are regularly presented under documentary credits are:

- bills of lading
    - marine or ocean
    - multimodal
    - container
    - charter party
    - short form (blank back)
    - received for shipment
    - non-negotiable sea waybills
- mate's receipt
- air waybills
- rail, road and inland waterway consignment notes
- parcel post receipts.

Of greatest importance to banks financing the movement of goods is their ability to obtain a title to them during transport and to transfer that title to a buyer upon liquidation of the finance. Only one transport document provides that security and that is the bill of lading.

The **marine or ocean bill of lading** performs a number of functions. It is a receipt for the goods detailed on its face, a contract of carriage, a negotiable document and evidence of the shipment of certain goods from a named port to a named port of destination. It should incorporate the following additional details:

- shipping company's name
- carrying vessel's name
- shipper's name
- marks and numbers of packages
- general description of goods
- name of consignee
- date of loading on board
- name of notify party
- number of original bills in the set
- signature of ship's master or shipping company's agent
- an indication of whether freight has been paid or is to be paid at destination
- contractual conditions of carriage (on reverse).

The bill of lading, because of its protective properties, is the most likely document to be rejected by banks due to faults in its issue, detrimental clauses which carriers add when packages appear damaged and presentation of incomplete sets (2 out of 3 originals). It is only a clean bill of lading if no detrimental clause appears on its face.

Multimodal bills of lading are issued to cover the transport of goods by at least two different modes from a point of departure by road, rail, barge or sea-going vessel for carriage to their destination. The essential feature of this document, required to make it acceptable within the terms of UCP600, is that at least one stage of the journey must be by sea.

Container bills of lading: nowadays many consignments by sea are made in containers. The container is packed at a port or an inland place of reception and may include goods from more than one exporter consigned to several buyers at destination. This is a very secure method as containers are specially sealed and coded to prevent theft and pilferage. The bill of lading is a receipt for the container at place of receipt and operates on a port-to-port basis, except that it can cover the goods from port of destination to an inland container depot; it is a full document of title.

Charterparty bills of lading evidence a contract between a vessel owner and a charterer who wishes to hire the vessel for a given period of time, not necessarily a specific journey. The reason for this is that charterers often purchase, for example, a cargo of oil before they have decided where it will be delivered. The document is known as a charter party and is subject to whatever terms have been agreed between the vessel owner and the charterer. It will be readily understood that the charterer has complete control over the goods and their ultimate destination which means that it provides no security for a bank financing the purchase. Although the charter party bill must indicate the ports of loading and discharge, it need not show the name of the carrier. Because charter party terms vary considerably depending on the nature of goods carried and journeys undertaken, banks are excused under Article 22b from examining their terms when a credit permits their presentation. Despite these shortcomings, this document is widely used for bulk cargoes and banks accept it provided they are dealing with buyers and sellers of undoubted standing.

Short form (or blank back) bills of lading do not include the full terms of the contract of carriage on the reverse side but in all other respects they fulfil the role of marine bills of lading.

Received for shipment bill of lading: this document is issued by the shipping company as a receipt for goods awaiting shipment. Once the goods are loaded, it will be stamped 'shipped on board'. It is not a document of title.

Non-negotiable sea waybills: in the same manner as ocean bills, this document acts as a receipt for goods and a contract of carriage. Its importance has increased due to the reduction in sea journey times, which often means that the carrying vessel arrives at its port of discharge before the bills of lading can be forwarded through the banking system. It is not a document of title and cannot therefore be used to transfer goods between parties. Goods covered by a sea waybill are destined for a named consignee to whom they will be released against suitable identification if the carrying vessel arrives at port of destination before the waybill. The use of waybills will increase with the development of electronic banking when title can be transferred through central registers.

Mate's receipt: The mate's receipt is issued as a receipt for goods awaiting shipment. It is not a document of title and is eventually exchanged for a 'shipped on board' bill of lading.

Air waybills act as a receipt for goods despatched by air, but are not negotiable and consequently not a document of title. The airline notifies and delivers the goods to the consignee. The air waybill offers no security to a bank financing the transaction unless the bank is shown as consignee. Understandably banks rarely agree to have goods consigned to them.

Rail, road or inland waterway transport documents are issued by hauliers or rail and canal operators. These are not documents of title as the goods go direct to the consignee.

Parcel post receipts as their name suggests are merely receipts for packages sent direct to a named consignee.

The **operation of a documentary credit** virtually reflects the contract between buyer and seller and traces the actual transaction through all stages up to delivery of the goods and payment to the seller. If we consider the specimen shown in Figure 4.3 we can analyse the credit and demonstrate how the parties fulfil their obligations.

The applicants: Universal Components Ltd have contracted to buy 140 metric tons of aluminium sheets at US$1400 per metric ton CFR Liverpool

from Nasas Aluminium Sanayi ve Ticareti SA.

The issuing bank: Mid Orient Bank, London has issued, in accordance with instructions from Universal Components Ltd an irrevocable credit No. 1560/001.

Amount: not exceeding US$196 000.

Expiry date: 31 August 2003 in Istanbul.

SPECIMEN

ISSUE OF A DOCUMENTARY CREDIT   **** SWIFT NORMAL ****

SENDER: *RECEIVER:*
MID ORIENT BANK, LONDON

---

* FORM OF DOCUMENTARY CREDIT *
IRREVOCABLE

* DOCUMENTARY CREDIT NUMBER *
1560/001

* DATE OF ISSUE *
01.04.01

* DATE AND PLACE OF EXPIRY *
ISTANBUL 31.08.01

* APPLICANT *
UNIVERSAL COMPONENTS LTD, BIRMINGHAM

* BENEFICIARY *
NASAS ALUMINIUM VE SANAYI TICARETI S.A.

* CURRENCY CODE, AMOUNT *
NOT EXCEEDING US$ 196 000

* AVAILABLE WITH TURKIYE AYDIN BANKASI *BY* PAYMENT AT SIGHT ***

* PARTIAL SHIPMENTS *
NOT ALLOWED

* TRANSHIPMENT *
NOT ALLOWED

* LOADING ON BOARD/DESPATCH/TAKING IN CHARGE AT /FROM *
ANY TURKISH PORT

* FOR TRANSPORTATION TO . . . . . *
LIVERPOOL UK, CFR

* LATEST DATE OF SHIPMENT *
16.08.01

* DESCRIPTION OF GOODS AND/OR SERVICES *
140 METRIC TONS ALUMINIUM SHEETS @ US$1400 PER MT, CFR LIVERPOOL

* DOCUMENTS REQUIRED *
SIGNED COMMERCIAL INVOICE IN TRIPLICATE
CERTIFICATE OF ORIGIN ISSUED BY THE CHAMBER OF COMMERCE
WEIGHT LIST IN DUPLICATE
QUALITY INSPECTION CERTIFICATE ISSUED BY CARGO SUPERINTENDENTS AT PORT
OF LOADING
FULL SET CLEAN ON BOARD OCEAN BILL OF LADING ISSUED TO ORDER, BLANK
ENDORSED MARKED 'NOTIFY UNIVERSAL COMPONENTS DATE FOUNDRY BIRMINGHAM'
AND STAMPED 'FREIGHT PAID'.

* ADDITIONAL CONDITIONS
INSURANCE COVERED BY BUYER

* CHARGES*
FOR ACCOUNT OF BUYER

* CONFIRMATION INSTRUCTIONS *
DO NOT CONFIRM

* REIMBURSEMENT BANK *
BANK OF AMERICA, NEW YORK

* SENDER TO RECEIVER INFORMATION *
PLEASE DRAW ON OUR ACCOUNT WITH BANK OF AMERICA, NEW YORK
UNDER SIMULTANEOUS TELEX ADVICE TO US

* INSTRUCTIONS TO PAYING/ACCEPTING/NEGOTIATING BANK *
DOCUMENTS TO BE FORWARDED TO US BY COURIER

Figure 4.3

Advising/nominated bank: Mid Orient Bank have appointed Turkiye Aydin Bankasi, Istanbul to authenticate the credit and advise it to the beneficiaries. That bank may, if it wishes, inform Nasas Aluminium that it is prepared to make payment in due course against compliant documents, i.e. to act as nominated bank. It is instructed not to confirm the credit.

The beneficiaries: Nasas Aluminium are not obliged to acknowledge receipt of the credit, but if any of its terms do not meet with their approval, they must revert to Universal Components and not to the advising or issuing banks.

Reimbursement bank: Bank of America are authorized to honour a claim for payment from Turkiye Aydin Bankasi and to debit the account in their books of Mid Orient Bank, London. They will have been given the essential details of the credit by Mid Orient.

General: Part shipments and transhipments are not allowed. Shipment is to be effected CFR (cost and freight). Documents required include a certificate of inspection issued by cargo superintendents at port of loading, so Nasas Aluminium will have to arrange that inspection is made immediately the goods are **sent to** the port of shipment. Turkiye Aydin Bankasi are instructed *not* to confirm the credit. If they are asked by the beneficiaries to add their confirmation, they must first seek the agreement of Mid Orient Bank. To confirm without their agreement would amount to a **silent** confirmation.

UCP600:   The credit is issued through Swift and is automatically subject to UCP600. Article 30b allows a tolerance of 5% more or less for goods shipped in bulk and applies to this credit. However, the cost of 140 metric tons at US$140 000 per metric ton CFR is US$196 000. The amount of the credit, US$196 000, cannot, in any circumstances, be exceeded and therefore the tolerance permitted under this credit is not exceeding 5% less than 140 metric tons (133 metric tons), i.e. 140 metric tons is the maximum tonnage permitted.

Assuming that no amendments to the credit are required, Nasas will eventually present the full set of documents for negotiation by Turkiye

Aydin Bankasi. If they are in order, the bank will pay the invoice amount, courier the documents to Mid Orient Bank, London and claim reimbursement from Bank of America, New York. Mid Orient will check the documents and if there are no discrepancies, release them to Universal Components.

Confirmation of a documentary credit

The beneficiary of a documentary credit may be reluctant to accept the risk that a bank in a foreign country will honour its engagement, particularly if the credit covers his first transaction with that country. He will be aware that in countries with economic problems and which are short of foreign exchange, the central bank may bar or delay payment under an import credit. The solution for the beneficiary is to ask for the credit to be confirmed by a bank in his own country. By adding its confirmation, the confirming bank undertakes that, provided the stipulated documents are presented to it **or to any other nominated bank** and that the terms and conditions of the credit have been complied with, it will:

1 Pay at sight for a sight credit.
2 Pay at maturity for a deferred payment credit.
3 Accept drafts under a usance credit and pay them at maturity.
4 Pay at maturity drafts drawn on another drawee bank but not paid by that bank at maturity.
5 Accept and pay at maturity drafts drawn on it by the beneficiary of a credit in replacement of drafts drawn on another bank but not accepted by it.
6 Negotiate drafts drawn by the beneficiary.

All the above undertakings are executed by the confirming bank **without** recourse to the beneficiary (Article 8).

Article 8 can be dangerous for a confirming bank as it obliges the bank to honour drafts drawn on it by the beneficiary if drafts drawn on another drawee bank stipulated in the credit are not accepted or accepted and not paid at maturity by that bank. Alternatively it may be obliged to honour drafts accepted by another drawee bank but not paid at maturity.

While the intention is right and demonstrates the responsibilities of confirmation, the confirming bank in its original undertaking to the beneficiary should state that it will honour drafts provided that they are presented with the relative documents in order within the validity of the credit. It can hardly be right for the confirming bank to be obliged to pay for documents which it has not had the opportunity to examine. Furthermore, if the first drawee bank refused to accept drafts drawn on it, by the time new drafts had been prepared and presented to the confirming bank the presentation time for the transport documents (Article 14c) will probably have expired.

These are considerable responsibilities undertaken by the bank, which indicate the seriousness of confirmation. Banks do not lightly add their confirmation to credits and will want to ensure that they limit to a minimum the possibility of loss. So far as the beneficiary is concerned the confirming bank is the end of the line; once it has paid, accepted a bill of exchange or given an undertaking to make a future payment, **it has no recourse against the beneficiary**. It follows that a bank considering a request to add its confirmation to a foreign bank's credit will pay strict attention to a number of its principal features.

1 Relationship, if any, with the issuing bank.
2 Term: sight, usance or deferred payment.
3 Expiry date.
4 Method of despatch.
5 Title to the goods.
6 Reimbursement clause.
7 Pre-shipment finance required.
8 Responsibility for its charges.

Finally, the bank will consider whether the beneficiary, if not already a customer, is worth approaching in order to develop a relationship; confirming a credit, particularly at the beneficiary's request may provide the necessary incentive.

The reader will appreciate the significant differences between a sight credit and one payable at a future date. A bank confirming a sight credit will expect reimbursement for any negotiation within a few days, but under a usance or deferred payment credit it may have to wait up to a year for the issuing bank to honour its undertaking. Confirmation is basically cover against political risks and assessing those risks for one year or more requires considerably more confidence in the issuing bank than for a short-term credit. By way of an example, a credit may be valid for 9 months, and during the last month of its validity the beneficiary presents his documents for negotiation. If it is a 365 day usance credit, the total period of exposure on the issuing bank will be 21 months. One has only to recall the failure of certain prominent banks in the past, plus the rapid economic decline of some countries, to appreciate the possible risks of confirming usance and deferred payment credits.

Most international banks provide facilities to foreign banks for confirming their credits, with limits on total outstandings and conditions as to the types of credits they will confirm. When requested by an issuing bank to add its confirmation to a credit, the nominated bank will generally agree, provided the facility conditions permit, and will advise the beneficiary that the credit carries its confirmation. Often it is the beneficiary who requests confirmation, in which case the nominated bank must ensure that the issuing bank does not expressly state that the credit is not to be confirmed. A nominated bank which ignores such an instruction risks damaging relations with the issuing bank. In cases where the issuing bank either allows confirmation or makes no particular stipulation about it, the nominated bank may accede to a request from the beneficiary for confirmation, but it should advise the issuing bank in case the confirmation has utilized part of a facility.

It is not always essential for a bank to confirm a credit for its full amount or, indeed, for its full validity. A nominated bank may not wish to confirm a credit for US$6 m valid for 12 months but may be prepared to confirm it to the extent of US$3 m for a period of 6 months. Confirming for a reduced amount is only possible if the credit permits part shipments, so there is no reason why a beneficiary cannot accept confirmation for a reduced amount, ship goods to that value and request confirmation of the balance when the confirming bank has received reimbursement.

Once it has added its confirmation, the confirming bank becomes a contractual party to the credit. It is in contract with the issuing bank and with the beneficiary to whom it has given its undertaking. Any amendment to the terms of the credit after confirmation can only be made with the agreement of the confirming bank. It is easy to understand that an amendment which increases the commitment of the confirming bank has to be assessed as a new risk and it may not wish to accept the amendment. Increases to the credit amount, extensions to validity and changes in term from sight to usance are examples of the type of amendments which may prompt a confirming bank to reject them or thereafter remove its confirmation if they are allowed.

Although it is thought that a confirming bank cannot escape its commitment once given, there is a way to remove its confirmation if it objects to certain amendments advised by the issuing bank. Article 9div states 'partial acceptance of amendments confirmed in one and the same advice of amendment is not allowed and consequently will not be given any effect'. For example, a confirming bank receives instructions from the issuing bank to effect the following amendments to a credit:

1 Increase amount by US$750 000.
2 Extend validity to 31 December 2003.

If it does not wish to increase its risk on the issuing bank it has only to add a third amendment as follows:

3 This credit no longer carries our confirmation.

The beneficiary has two options: firstly to leave the credit as it stands unamended, or secondly to accept *all* the amendments and lose the confirmation.

Silent confirmation

When an issuing bank sends a credit to its nominated bank it will usually include instructions regarding confirmation. These instructions are in three forms:

1 please add your confirmation, or
2 do not add your confirmation, or
3 you may add your confirmation.

Alternatively, the credit may omit any reference whatsoever to confirmation.

Firstly, if the nominated bank is requested to add it's confirmation, it is not obliged to do so. However, if it does decline, it must immediately inform the issuing bank.

Secondly, if the nominated bank ignores an instruction *not* to confirm and decides to do so without advising the issuing bank, it effectively makes an **unauthorized amendment** to the credit.

Thirdly, where the nominated bank is given the option, it must still advise the issuing bank if it decides to confirm a credit.

Finally, where the issuing bank makes no reference to confirmation, it is still necessary for the nominated bank to advise it of any decision to confirm.

Silent confirmation therefore is any unauthorized confirmation of an irrevocable documentary credit by which a silent confirmer assumes **primary responsibility** for paying, accepting or issuing a deferred payment undertaken under a credit issued by a bank with whom it has no contractual relationship.

Why is it important to the beneficiary to have a credit confirmed?

1 If it is a **sight** credit he can be certain that he will be paid upon presentation of documents, in his own country and in his own currency.
2 If it is a **usance** credit the confirming bank can accept a draft upon presentation of documents and immediately discount it. The advantage of that process over the practice of sending drafts to the issuing bank for acceptance is obvious.
3 If the credit is expressed in a foreign currency the ability to discount as shown in (2) reduces the period of exchange risk to the beneficiary and may also enable him to escape a rise in interest rates.

4 Any payment/acceptance/undertaking by the confirming bank is made **without recourse to the beneficiary.**

The circumstances which may bring about the silent confirmation of a credit are:

1 The beneficiary may request the nominated bank to add its confirmation but although the issuing bank has either authorized confirmation or has made no mention of it, the nominated bank declines to assume the risk on the issuing bank. In that situation it is not uncommon for the beneficiary to approach another bank and request it to confirm the credit. If it does so, that bank is a silent confirmer, unless it takes the precaution of obtaining the agreement of the issuing bank.
2 Although expressly forbidden to confirm a credit, the nominated bank may decide to ignore that instruction and accede to the beneficiary's request for confirmation.

Both (1) and (2) can result in a silent confirmation.

What are the risks to the silent confirmer?

1 Political
   - Adding confirmation to a credit against the wishes of the issuing bank could seriously damage relations with that bank.
   - In some countries, it is forbidden for their credits to be confirmed by third party banks – the risk is obvious!
   - Where confirmation lines accorded to some countries are strictly limited for sovereign reasons, using part of those lines for silent confirmation could seriously embarrass both the issuing and confirming bank.
2 Technical
   - If the silent confirmer is not the advising/nominated bank, it will have to rely on the beneficiary to provide an up-to-date record of the credit and any amendments which have already been made.
   - As the issuing bank is unaware of the silent confirmer, it will continue to direct amendments and correspondence to the advising/nominated

bank. Even if the silent confirmer has an agreement with the advising/nominated bank for all amendments to be routed through themselves instead of advising them direct to the beneficiary, an oversight can occur.

- The silent confirmer thus faces the possibility that:
  - the credit could be amended without its knowledge or approval
  - the beneficiary could signify his agreement to an amendment which may be quite unacceptable to the silent confirmer who, having no contractual relationship with the issuing bank, cannot object to it
  - if the issuing bank discovers that the credit has been confirmed without its agreement, it may regard it as an unauthorized amendment
  - the reimbursing agent appointed by the issuing bank may refuse a claim from a silent confirmer, as it may only be authorized to reimburse the advising/nominated bank.

So why do it?

1 The beneficiary may be a customer or a good potential customer.
2 The income to the silent confirmer can be considerable.
3 The beneficiary may be indebted to the silent confirmer, who sees an opportunity to get his hands on the credit proceeds to reduce the debt.
4 The silent confirmer may be able to avail itself of telegraphic reimbursement on a reimbursing agent. Thus it could be in funds before the issuing bank can raise any objection to the confirmation.
5 The beneficiary may subsequently persuade his foreign buyers to route future credits through the silent confirmer with obvious benefits to that bank.

Conclusion

Despite the risks, the practice of silent confirmation is very prevalent and generally demonstrates the skills and competitiveness of the banks involved.

Amendments to the terms of an irrevocable credit

Amendments require the agreement of all the parties, applicant, issuing bank, beneficiary and confirming bank if the credit is confirmed. The applicant is responsible for instructing the issuing bank to effect an amendment and is generally responding to a request from the beneficiary who considers the credit is not entirely as agreed in his contract. Most common is the extension to the latest shipment date and the validity. It is worth mentioning here that the applicant may sometimes limit the validity of a credit to, say, 6 months whereas the contract of sale stipulated 9 months. By reducing the validity he also reduces the opening commission by one third and probably hopes the beneficiary will be persuaded to effect shipment earlier than intended. When a beneficiary receives a credit which is not precisely what he contracted for, he must immediately request the necessary amendment from the applicant. If he delays and then finds himself unable to execute his part of the contract within its terms, the market may have moved against him with the result that the buyer can allow the credit to expire unutilized and find a cheaper supplier or agree to an extension to the credit and demand a discount on the original price.

For example, whereas a nominated bank may have been prepared to add its confirmation to a sight credit for, say, US$3 000 000, it might take a different view if the issuing bank subsequently amended the term to usance at 180 days sight. There is a significant difference in the period of risk. If the confirming bank decides that it does not want to be liable under the amended usance credit, it can simply send an advice to the beneficiary worded as follows:

1 This credit is now available against drafts drawn at 180 days sight.
2 Our confirmation is withdrawn.

The confirming bank is taking advantage of Article 10e which obliges any beneficiary to either accept all or reject all amendments included in the **one advice**.

It would be correct for the confirming bank to advise the issuing bank of its decision.

Credits are frequently amended in a manner which appears to adversely affect the beneficiary; for example, a reduction in the amount of a credit or in the price of the goods. However, Article 10c states that a beneficiary should give notification of acceptance or rejection of amendment(s) but if he fails to give notification the only way the nominated or issuing bank will know whether he has accepted or rejected will be when he eventually presents documents. If they conform to the original credit terms it is understood the amendment has been rejected and vice versa.

Although Article 10c gives the beneficiary the option of notifying acceptance or rejection of an amendment or remaining silent until he presents his documents, the position of the issuing and confirming bank, if any, can be frustrating.

If we consider the amendments mentioned above, whereby a credit is amended from sight to 180 days usance and if the beneficiary does not accept or reject the amendment advice:

1 The issuing bank does not know whether it is liable under a sight or usance credit.
2 If the credit is confirmed, the confirming bank has to consider that *it could still be liable* under a sight credit.
3 In addition, the confirming bank will continue to record a risk against the issuing bank for the amount of the credit, thereby using up a valuable facility.

If the amendment had been a reduction from an amount of US$3 000 000 to US$2 000 000 the issuing bank and the confirming bank would be obliged to block facilities for US$3 000 000 until presentation of documents by the beneficiary.

Advising, nominated or confirming banks should always at least ask the beneficiary to acknowledge receipt of an amendment and to signify acceptance or rejection in the hopes of obtaining a reply.

Recourse

UCP600 does not state positively in what situations a negotiating, paying or accepting bank, or one giving an undertaking under a deferred payment credit has recourse to the beneficiary. But it does state, in Article 8ii that confirming banks can only pay, negotiate, accept or give undertakings **without recourse**. By inference, therefore, in all other situations nominated and non-confirming banks do have recourse to the beneficiary when paying, negotiating, accepting or giving undertakings.

It is hard to believe that a bank can accept a bill of exchange under a credit and yet still have recourse to the drawer (the beneficiary). But it is a fact that a nominated bank can, with the authority of the issuing bank, accept a bill of exchange under that bank's credit. If it has not confirmed the credit, the nominated bank will accept the bill 'with recourse'.

Any sensible bank asked to act as a nominated bank and to accept bills under another bank's credit will either decline to act as accepting bank or will insist on confirming the credit (provided that the issuing bank is an acceptable risk). A bank asked to add its confirmation to a credit and able to accept the risk on the issuing bank should amend the credit so that the bills of exchange are drawn on itself.

The reasons and benefits are obvious.

1 Acceptance by the confirming bank is immediate whereas acceptance by the issuing bank may take 7–14 days.
2 The accepted bill can be discounted immediately by the confirming or any other bank, with obvious advantages to the beneficiary.
3 The confirming bank will additionally earn acceptance commission and discount charges.
4 It can use the transaction to establish a relationship with the beneficiary, who has received his payment considerably earlier than if the bill had been drawn on the issuing bank.

The profitability of confirmation is not without risk for, as stated earlier, the confirming bank has no recourse to the beneficiary. Thus, a technical error made in examining documents could result in refusal by the issuing bank, leaving the confirming bank at the mercy of the importer (applicant).

Deferred payment credits

UCP600 has at last clarified the position of banks who are asked to negotiate deferred payment credits and to immediately discount the eventual payments. Article 7c states that reimbursement will be made "whether or not the nominated bank prepaid or purchased before maturity", which presumably means discounting. However, the Article refers only to the Nominated Bank, so other banks asked to discount would be well advised to seek agreement from the Issuing Bank before prepaying a Deferred Payment Credit.

The case which had cast doubts on the advisability of discounting documents negotiated under a deferred payment credit is Banco Santander SA and Banque Paribas (Court of Appeal, 2000). Paribas issued a deferred payment credit requiring the beneficiaries to present documents at the counters of Banco Santander in London. The credit stipulated that payment was to be deferred until 180 days from the date of the bill of lading. Banco Santander added their confirmation to the credit and at the same time offered the possibility of discounting. Documents eventually presented were determined by Banco Santander to be in order and accordingly it issued its undertaking to pay. Paribas and Santander became liable therefore to effect payment on 27 November, 1998. Documents were negotiated and discounted by Santander on 15 June; on 24 June, Paribas advised them that some of them were forged. On 27 November, Paribas refused to reimburse Santander.

The purpose of mentioning this case is to demonstrate the maxim that if an issuing or confirming bank is made aware of fraud **before effecting payment**, then payment cannot be made.

The Santander case drew a distinction between acceptance and discount of a draft by a confirming bank under a usance credit and discount of a deferred payment undertaking issued under a deferred payment credit. The Court of Appeal upheld the original judgement and allowed Paribas to withhold payment to Santander.

A subsequent case in Singapore (Banque Nationale de Paris v. Credit Agricole Indosuez, June, 2000) dealt with a credit stated to be 'available against presentation of drafts at 180 days from date of negotiation by deferred payment'. The reader will remember that issuing banks have a duty to avoid ambiguity in their credits. In this case, the words 'by deferred payment' were clearly unnecessary and gave rise to the claim by the issuing bank that it was not a usance credit. The Court's decision was that the confirming bank was entitled to treat the credit as usance and to be reimbursed on maturity of the 180 day drafts. If there is a moral in this story it is that, as stated earlier, advising banks should clarify with the issuing bank any doubtful wording in a credit which they intend to confirm.

Handling discrepant documents

Unfortunately, a high percentage of documents presented under documentary credits are out of order for one or more reasons. The negotiating bank is obliged to refuse discrepant documents but, depending on the seriousness of the discrepancies, there are a number of actions it can take in order to assist the beneficiary while at the same time ensuring that it avoids any action of which the issuing bank may disapprove.

Before considering how to deal with documents which do not comply with the terms of a credit, mention must be made of an important point. Until payment or acceptance of a bill of exchange by an issuing or confirming bank, all documents remain the property of the beneficiary. We can now examine the roles of those banks who form the chain in processing documents from the time of negotiation to final release to the applicant.

The negotiating bank

The negotiating bank, whether it is an advising, nominated, confirming or simply any bank negotiating a freely negotiable credit, must examine the documents presented to it and must decide **within a maximum of 5 days** whether to accept or reject them. It is important to understand that the 5 days is only a guideline because in many cases it would be difficult for a bank to claim that it had needed that long to examine a set of documents; some documents can be examined in 20 minutes, others may take many hours.

Examining documents is a skill which, unfortunately, is not given the recognition it deserves. A bank's money is at risk if a document-checker fails to detect a discrepancy when negotiating a credit. This is an appropriate point to consider the question of **recourse**. A negotiating bank which has no contractual relationship with the beneficiary, in other words, is neither the issuing nor confirming bank, negotiates **with recourse** to the beneficiary. This means that if, for any reason, the issuing bank does not reimburse it, the negotiating bank has the right to reclaim its payment from the beneficiary. The cynic will argue that getting money back from a beneficiary is unlikely, but the right of recourse can form the basis of a legal action if necessary. Any payment or acceptance by a confirming or an issuing bank can only be made **without recourse**. This illustrates the irrevocability of their undertaking; if a discrepancy is found in documents after payment or acceptance, they are faced with a loss if the applicant refuses them.

When documents are presented to a negotiating bank and are found to be out of order, there are five courses of action available to the bank.

1. Return them to the beneficiary for correction

When returning documents for correction, the negotiating bank must remind the beneficiary if expiry of the credit is imminent. Presentation of discrepant documents is a non-presentation and only when they have been put in order and re-presented **within the validity of the credit** can the documents be valid for negotiation. Sometimes the negotiating bank is unable to complete its examination of the documents before expiry of the credit, but providing examination takes no longer than the permitted 7 working days it will only be necessary to confirm to the issuing bank that documents, in order, were presented **within the validity date**.

2. Offer to pay or accept against a bank's indemnity to be supplied by the beneficiary

Providing the negotiating bank with an indemnity issued by an acceptable bank is often the quickest way in which a beneficiary can obtain payment or acceptance when his documents are found to be out of order. This arrangement is made solely between the negotiating bank and the beneficiary; the issuing bank is advised that the negotiating bank holds an indemnity and must decide itself whether to accept the discrepancies after referring back to the applicant, or to refuse them. It must be emphasized that the credit is the issuing bank's instrument and that it can still refuse discrepant documents **even if the applicant agrees to accept them**. This is an example of the issuing bank asserting its rights; it has the final say and may have doubts about the ability or willingness of the applicant to pay for the documents.

3. Offer to pay under reserve

Payment under reserve is an established practice employed by negotiating banks when the beneficiary is either a good customer or an undoubted corporate entity. The beneficiary is advised of the discrepancies discovered and is allowed to take payment on the understanding that if the issuing bank does not accept the documents, the payment must be refunded to the negotiating bank. It is important that the full meaning of payment under reserve is included in the payment advice. In Banque de L'Indochine et de Suez v. Rayner (Mincing Lane, 1981) the beneficiaries claimed they were unaware of their obligation to refund monies paid under reserve. In his finding the judge was critical of the fact that in London such payments were often agreed by telephone and relied on the goodwill of both parties, the bank and beneficiary. Although accepting the bank's assurance that payment under reserve was commonly made in that manner, he strongly advised that negotiating banks should set out the full implications in their advice to the beneficiary.

4. Contact the issuing bank and ask for authority to pay despite the discrepancies

Probably the best course open to a negotiating bank which realises that documents cannot be corrected, is to seek authority from the issuing bank to pay despite the discrepancies. The discrepancies, in full, are set out in a request to the issuing bank for authority to pay. This is another example of the risks involved in negotiating other bank's credits, for if the issuing bank authorizes payment and then discovers further discrepancies when it receives the actual documents, it will demand repayment of its reimbursement.

5. Send the documents for collection

In cases where the documents are hopelessly out of order the negotiating bank may feel that rather than list a whole string of irregularities, it should allow the issuing bank to examine the documents on a collection basis. But care must be taken to inform the issuing bank that the documents are being sent for collection under the credit and therefore in accordance with the terms of UCP600 *not* Uniform Rules for Collections. Failure to make that stipulation on the part of the negotiating bank can cost the beneficiary dearly.

It is not uncommon to see in an irrevocable credit the clause 'on no account will irregular documents be accepted'. This is a clear warning to negotiating banks that they are probably handling a transferred or back-to-back credit and that they accept any discrepancies at their peril. A negotiating bank which does its job properly should strongly advise any beneficiary against submitting an indemnity with documents under a credit bearing the clause mentioned above, as refusal by the issuing bank is virtually certain.

The issuing bank

For discrepant documents, their arrival at the issuing bank is the end of the line. If they are rejected, they are considered as being outside the credit. When documents are received and are found to be out of order, or their irregularities have already been notified by the negotiating bank, the issuing bank must determine what action to take. First and foremost, the credit is the issuing bank's own instrument and contains its irrevocable undertaking to the beneficiary. It therefore has the right to refuse or accept documents without consulting its customer, the applicant. But the whole purpose of a documentary credit is to provide a means of settling a contract between a buyer and a seller and it would be imprudent not to refer to the applicant when in receipt of discrepant documents. The bank has a maximum of 5 days in which to examine the documents, refer to the applicant and respond to the negotiating bank. In most cases, if the discrepancies are not serious and if the applicant is an honest buyer, he will waive them. The issuing bank will then honour the negotiating bank's claim for reimbursement.

If the applicant refuses to accept irregular documents then the issuing bank must advise the negotiating bank without delay and must inform it that the unaccepted documents are held at its disposal. It has been mentioned before that throughout these proceedings the documents remain the property of the beneficiary. Consequently, if the applicant changes his mind a few days after refusing the documents, the issuing bank cannot release them to him without the beneficiary's agreement. A worried beneficiary, believing he may not be paid, could have found an alternative buyer to whom the discrepant documents are acceptable.

Negotiation

Ever since the documentary credit became widely used, there have been controversy and arguments as to what constitutes negotiation. By advancing money to the beneficiary of another bank's credit, a negotiating bank takes considerable risks. The risks vary depending upon the standing of the issuing bank and the importing country; any bank requested to negotiate a set of documents must assess those risks.

UCP500 described negotiation as follows; "negotiation means the giving of value for drafts and/or documents by the bank authorized to negotiate". But the expression "giving of value" was not clearly explained and, in fact, was open to several interpretations, such as

- present: for immediate payment under a sight credit
- past: for advances already made; for example, the beneficiary may be a customer of the negotiating bank and could have asked for an advance against his documents which he deposited with them as security awaiting the issue of the bills of lading by the shipping company
- future: for undertakings given but not yet realised. By agreement with the beneficiary, the negotiating bank makes payment only when it has been reimbursed by the issuing bank, rather than risk advancing its own cash.

Understandably, a bank which is not the confirming bank will wish to exercise caution when asked to negotiate documents under a foreign bank's credit. It cannot be certain that it will be reimbursed for any advance it makes, but at the same time it may wish to assist the beneficiary, who could be its customer, in obtaining payment. In some cases the credit may be close to expiry, leaving the beneficiary little opportunity to present the documents to the confirming or issuing bank with any hope of correcting them if they are found to be out of order. So, acting cautiously, the negotiating bank may decide to take a line between running a risk itself and providing a solution to the beneficiary's problem. It agrees to negotiate, but to pay the beneficiary only after receipt of reimbursement from the issuing bank. According to Article 10bii this procedure did not constitute a negotiation but if the negotiating bank took no action the credit would expire leaving the beneficiary without any rights against the issuing bank. In the Far East this practice is widespread and has been practised for many years. In Banque Indosuez v. Indian Bank (Singapore, 1992) it was held that 'value was given, although the beneficiary agreed to be paid after receipt of cover', i.e. following reimbursement by the issuing bank. Now UCP600 has dropped the expression "giving of value" and Article 2 permits the advancing or agreeing to advance funds to the beneficiary on or before the banking day on which reimbursement is due to the nominated bank.

Although UCP600 will suggest that only the nominated bank may negotiate, sensible banks will always weigh the risks of negotiating against the need to assist their customers; in so doing they contribute towards the smooth completion of contracts involving the movement of goods across the world, which is the whole purpose of a documentary credit.

Article 8. Revocation of a credit

(a) A revocable credit may be amended or cancelled by the issuing bank at any moment and without prior notice to the beneficiary.

Article 9. Liability of issuing and confirming banks

(a) An irrevocable credit constitutes a definite undertaking of the issuing bank, provided that the stipulated documents are presented to the

Articles 7 and 8. Liability of issuing and confirming banks.

Provided that the stipulated documents are presented and constitute a complying presentation, the issuing and confirming bank must honor them if the credit is available by:

(i) sight payment, deferred payment or acceptance.

(ii) sight payment with a nominated bank and that bank does not pay.

(iii) deferred payment with a nominated bank and that bank does not incur its deferred undertaking or, having incurred its deferred payment undertaking, does not pay at maturity.

(iv) acceptance with a nominated bank and that bank does not accept a draft drawn on it or, having accepted a draft drawn on it, does not pay at maturity.

(v) negotiation with a nominated bank and that bank does not negotiate. An issuing bank is irrevocably bound to honor as of the time that it issues the credit. A confirming bank is irrevocably bound to honor or negotiate as of the time it adds it's confirmation.

Article 10. Amendments

(a) Except as otherwise provided by Article 38, a credit can neither be amended nor cancelled without the agreement of the issuing bank.

(b) An issuing bank is irrevocably bound by an amendment as of the time it issues the amendment. A confirming bank may extend its confirmation to an amendment and will be irrevocably bound as of the time it issues the amendment.
A confirming bank may, however, choose to advise an amendment to the beneficiary without extending its confirmation and if so, must inform the issuing bank and the beneficiary without delay.

(c) The terms of the original credit (or a credit incorporating previously accepted amendment(s)) will remain in force for the beneficiary until the beneficiary communicates his acceptance of the amendment to the bank that advised such amendment. The beneficiary should give notification of acceptance or rejection of amendment(s). If the beneficiary fails to give such notification, the tender of documents to the nominated bank or issuing bank, that conform to the credit and to not yet accepted amendment(s), will be deemed to be notification of acceptance by the beneficiary of such amendment(s) and as of that moment the credit will be amended.

(d) Partial acceptance of amendments contained in one and the same advice of amendment is not allowed and consequently will not be given any effect.

Article 10. Types of credit

(a) All credits must clearly indicate whether they are available by sight payment, by deferred payment, by acceptance or by negotiation.

(b) (i) Unless the credit stipulates that it is available only with the issuing bank, all credits must nominate the bank (the 'Nominated bank') which is authorized to pay, to incur a deferred payment undertaking, to accept draft(s) or to negotiate. In a freely negotiable credit, any bank is a nominated bank. Presentation of documents must be made to the issuing bank or the confirming bank, if any, or any other nominated bank.

(ii) Negotiation means the giving of value for draft(s) and/or document(s) by the bank authorized to negotiate. Mere examination of the documents without giving of value does not constitute a negotiation.

Article 14. Standard for examination of documents

The issuing bank, the confirming bank, if any, or a nominated bank acting on their behalf, shall each have a reasonable time, not to exceed 5 banking days following the day of receipt of the documents, to examine the documents and determine whether to take up or refuse the documents and to inform the party from which it received the documents accordingly.

If a credit contains conditions without stating the document(s) to be presented in compliance therewith, banks will deem such conditions as not stated and will disregard them.

Article 16. Discrepant documents and notice

(a) Upon receipt of documents, the issuing and/or confirming bank, if any, or a nominated bank acting on their behalf, must determine on the basis of the documents alone, whether or not they appear on their face to be in compliance with terms and conditions of the credit. If the documents appear on their face not to be in compliance with the terms and conditions of the credit, such banks may refuse to take up the documents.

(i)   to reimburse the nominated bank which has paid, incurred a deferred payment undertaking, accepted draft(s), or negotiated;

(ii) to take up the documents.

If the issuing bank determines that the documents appear on their face not to be in compliance with the terms and conditions of the credit, it may in its sole judgement approach the applicant for a waiver of the discrepancy(ies).

If the issuing bank and/or confirming bank, if any, or a nominated bank acting on their behalf, decides to refuse the documents, it must give notice to that effect by telecommunication or, if that is not possible, by other expeditious means, without delay but not later than the close of the seventh banking day following the day of receipt of the documents. Such notice shall be given to the bank from which it received the documents, or to the beneficiary, if it received the documents directly from him.

Such notice must state all discrepancies in respect of which the bank refuses the documents and must also state whether it is holding the documents at the disposal of, or is returning them to, the presenter.

If the issuing bank and/or confirming bank, if any, fails to act in accordance with the provisions of this Article and/or fails to hold the documents at the disposal of, or return them to the presenter, the issuing bank and/or confirming bank, if any, shall be precluded from claiming that the documents are not in compliance with the terms and conditions of the credit.

Article 20. Marine/ocean bill of lading and Article 21, non-negotiable sea waybill

Both referred to as a document, however named which:

(i)   appears on its face to indicate the name of the carrier and to have been signed or otherwise authenticated by:

- the carrier or a named agent for or on behalf of the carrier; or
- the master as a named agent for or on behalf of the master.

Any signature or authentication of the carrier or master must be identified as carrier or master, as the case may be. An agent signing or authenticating for the carrier or master must also indicate the name of the capacity of the party, i.e. carrier or master, on whose behalf that agent is acting, and

(ii)   indicates that the goods have been loaded on board, or shipped on a named vessel. Loading on board or shipment on a named vessel may be indicated by pre-printed wording on the bill of lading, that the goods have been loaded on board a named vessel or shipped on a named vessel, in which case the date of issuance of the bill of lading will be deemed to be the date of loading on board and the date of shipment.

In all other cases loading on board a named vessel must be evidenced by a notation on the bill of lading which gives the date on which the goods have been loaded on board, in which case the date of the on board notation will be deemed to be the date of shipment.

If the bill of lading contains the indication 'intended vessel', or similar qualification in relation to the vessel, loading on board a named vessel must be evidenced by an on board notation on the bill of lading which, in addition to the date on which the goods have been loaded on board, also includes the name of the vessel on which the goods have been loaded, even if they have been loaded on the vessel named as the 'intended vessel'. If the bill of lading indicates a place of receipt or taking in charge different from the port of loading, the on board notation must also include the port of loading stipulated in the credit and the name of the vessel on which the goods have been loaded, even if they have been loaded on the vessel named in the bill of lading. This provision also applies whenever loading on board the vessel is indicated by pre-printed wording on the bill of lading.

Article 22. Charter party bill of lading

A document, however named, which:

(i)   contains any indication that it is subject to a charter party, and

(ii)   appears on its face to have been signed or otherwise authenticated by:

- the master or a named agent for or on behalf of the master, or
- the owner or a named agent for or on behalf of the owner.

Any signature or authentication of the master or owner must be identified as master or owner as the case may be. An agent signing or authenticating for the master or owner must also indicate the name and the capacity of the party, i.e. master or owner, on whose behalf that agent is acting, and

(iii) does or does not indicate the name of the carrier.

Article 19. Multimodal transport document

A document, however named, which covers at least two different modes of transport and:

(i) appears on its face to indicate the name of the carrier or multimodal transport operator and to have been signed or otherwise authenticated by:

● the carrier or multimodal transport operator or a named agent for or on behalf of the carrier or multimodal transport operator, or

● the master or a named agent for or on behalf of the master.

Any signature or authentication of the carrier, multimodal transport operator or master must be identified as carrier, multimodal transport operator or master, as the case may be. An agent signing or authenticating for the carrier, multimodal transport operator or master must also indicate the name and the capacity of the party, i.e. carrier, multimodal transport operator or master, on whose behalf that agent is acting.

(ii) indicates that the goods have been despatched, taken in charge or loaded on board.

Article 24. Road, rail or inland waterway transport documents

A document, however named, which:

(i) appears on its face to indicate the name of the carrier and to have been signed or otherwise authenticated by the carrier or a named agent for or on behalf of the carrier and/or to bear a reception stamp or other indication of receipt by the carrier or a named agent for or on behalf of the carrier.

Any signature, authentication, reception stamp or other indication of receipt of the carrier, must be identified on its face as that of the carrier. An agent signing or authenticating for the carrier must also indicate the name and the capacity of the party, i.e. carrier, on whose behalf that agent is acting.

Article 30. Allowances in credit amount, quantity and unit price

(i) The words 'about', 'approximately', 'circa' or similar expressions used in connection with the amount of the Credit of the quantity or the unit price stated in the Credit are to be construed as allowing a difference not to exceed 10% more or 10% less than the amount or the quantity or the unit price to which they refer.

(ii) Unless a Credit stipulates that the quantity of the goods specified must not be exceeded or reduced, a tolerance of 5% more or 5% less will be permissible, always provided that the amount of the drawings does not exceed the amount of the Credit. This tolerance does not apply when the Credit stipulates the quantity in terms of a stated number of packing units or individual items.

(iii) Unless a Credit which prohibits partial shipments stipulates otherwise, or unless sub-Article (ii) above is applicable, a tolerance of 5% less in the amount of the drawing will be permissible, provided that if the Credit stipulates the quantity of the goods, such quantity of foods is shipped in full, and if the Credit stipulates a unit price, such price is not reduced. This provision does not apply when expressions referred to in sub-Article (i) above are used in the Credit.

Chapter 5

Guarantees

Types of guarantee

Guarantees, or bonds as they are otherwise known, are widely used in international trade to support performance and payment obligations. Before examining the various instruments which are issued to provide a form of security for importers and exporters, it is necessary to distinguish between the two basic types of guarantee.

The **true guarantee** is used when a guarantor undertakes to be responsible for the debt or debts of a third party. A simple example is where a father guarantees his son's borrowings from a bank. The essential feature of this guarantee, which sets it apart from the on-demand guarantee, is the fact that the guarantor is **secondarily** liable. The beneficiary cannot call for payment under the guarantee until he can show that he has first requested repayment of the debt from the principal, without success (Fig. 5.1).

The **on-demand guarantee** is an undertaking by a bank to pay the beneficiary a certain sum to cover the action or default of a third party. A government department may engage a contractor to build a bridge but will require some sort of guarantee against faulty work and delay. On behalf of the contractor, a bank issues a performance guarantee for a percentage of the contract value which will compensate the buyer if the contractor defaults. In this form of guarantee, the guarantor is **primarily** liable; the beneficiary has only to make a demand, worded precisely as indicated in the guarantee and he will be paid. Banks do not concern themselves with

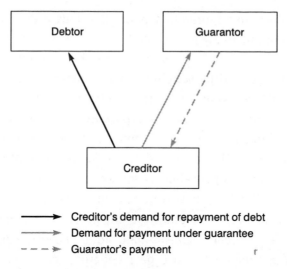

Creditor's demand for repayment of debt
Demand for payment under guarantee
Guarantor's payment

Guarantor only becomes liable when creditor's demand for repayment of debt has been ignored by the debtor.

Figure 5.1 True guarantee

disputes between the buyer and seller and even when a seller attempts to prevent a bank from meeting a claim under its on-demand guarantee by seeking a court injunction, it is rarely granted. The reason is obvious: bank guarantees, used internationally, must be seen to be quite independent of the underlying transaction.

The principal types of guarantees used in international trade are:

1 Bid bonds.
2 Performance bonds.
3 Retention bonds.
4 Advance payment bonds.

Before describing their roles it will be of assistance to consider the stages of a typical contract and the point at which each bond comes into use.

A government department in, say, Egypt issues an invitation for tenders to supply 20 000 tons of wheat. Notice of this invitation is advertised internationally and includes the terms of tender. As a rule, suppliers wishing to tender are required to support their bids with a bid bond issued by a bank acceptable to the buyer. The bond will be for 5% of the total value of the bid and is intended to ensure that the bid is genuine and correctly calculated. The successful supplier whose tender wins the contract is normally asked to provide a performance bond, generally for 10% of the contract value. This bond serves two purposes: it exerts pressure on the supplier to perform or lose his 10% and it provides compensation for the foreign government if the supplier defaults and an alternative supplier has to be found. That compensation is known as liquidated damages. As a further security, the foreign government may demand a retention bond which allows it to claim a refund from any amount paid to the supplier if the wheat is found to be sub-standard after delivery. For his part, the supplier may ask for an advance payment from the foreign government, often up to 10% of the contract value. If an advance is agreed, the supplier has to provide an advance payment bond.

Bid bonds

The **bid bond** (Fig. 5.2) accompanies any bid by a supplier or contractor seeking to win a contract abroad which has been put out to tender. Such contracts are often offered by buyers, generally government departments, seeking to purchase large quantities of commodities or to initiate a major construction undertaking such as the installation of a desalination plant or the building of a bridge. Suppliers are invited to submit their tenders, or bids as they are commonly known. The tenders must be submitted by a fixed closing date and be accompanied by an acceptable bid bond. When all the bids have been examined and the contract is awarded to the successful bidder his bid bond is withheld by the principal until he provides a performance guarantee and any other undertaking required under the terms of the contract. It is important to understand that it is a very expensive procedure for an overseas buyer to set up an invitation for tenders which is advertised throughout the world. For that reason, the buyer cannot afford to allow a supplier to walk away from a contract once it has been awarded to him. He may have made an error in calculating his price and realises that he will lose money if he completes the contract, but unless the error is greater than the amount of the bid bond he is obliged to honour his agreement. As an added measure to prevent default, many government buyers and institutions have introduced a clause in their requests for tenders which states that the bid bond provided by the successful bidder will automatically be converted into a performance bond for 10% of the contract value. For 5% of the contract amount, a bid bond does not normally present a serious risk to the issuing bank. The customer is bidding against a large number of competitors and the bank will only issue the bond if the customer is experienced in the trade and competent to carry out the contract if his bid is successful.

However, a 10% performance bond may be beyond the level of facilities which the bank extends to its customer and consequently, when agreeing to issue a 5% bid bond, the bank should advise the customer if it is not prepared to issue the required performance bond, even if his bid is successful. Obviously, where the terms of the tender are that the successful bid bond will automatically be converted into a performance bond, the

---

We understand that . . . . are tendering for the supply of . . . . under your Bid invitation No. . . . . of . . . . and that in accordance with the tender conditions a Bank Guarantee is required for . . . . % of the amount of their tender.

We . . . . hereby guarantee the payment to you on first demand of up to . . . . in the event of your awarding the relative contract to . . . . and of their failing to sign the contract awarded to them, or of their withdrawing their tender before expiry of this guarantee without your consent.

The total amount of this guarantee will be reduced by any payment effected hereunder.

For the purpose of identification, your request for payment in writing must bear the confirmation of your bankers that the signatories thereon are authorized so to sign.

This guarantee shall expire at close of banking hours at this office
On . . . . (in words . . . .)

If your claim has not been made on or before that date, regardless of such date being a banking date or not, this guarantee shall become null and void whether returned to us for cancellation or not. Any claim or statement received after expiry shall be ineffective.

This guarantee is goverened by . . . . law, place of jurisdiction is . . . .

Figure 5.2 Specimen bid bond

issuing bank has to either accept the potential risk of 10% or decline to issue the bid bond at the outset.

Performance bonds

The **performance bond** (Fig. 5.3) is demanded by overseas buyers or principals who do not wish to rely entirely on the expertise, financial strength or track record of the contractor. They want to be certain that if a contractor defaults or fails in any way to carry out the contract, they will be financially compensated for the resultant loss. The bond does not guarantee that the supplier or contractor will complete the transaction, or that if he fails the bank will find an alternative contractor; it simply provides for payment of liquidated damages on financial assessment of the principal's loss. Issuing performance guarantees involves banks in assuming considerable risks: their customer may fail, a technical dispute may result in the bond being called and they may be involved in unfair calling by the beneficiary. In common with all the bonds we are considering, the performance bond is payable on demand, a fact which has placed a serious

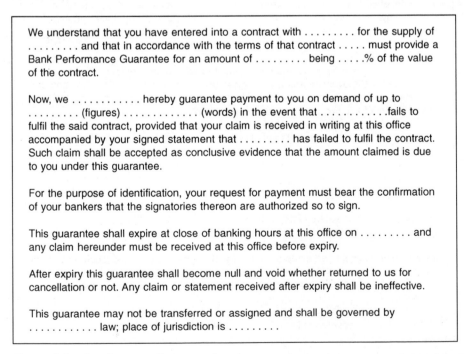

We understand that you have entered into a contract with . . . . for the supply of
. . . . and that in accordance with the terms of that contract . . . . . must provide a
Bank Performance Guarantee for an amount of . . . . being . . . . .% of the value
of the contract.

Now, we . . . . hereby guarantee payment to you on demand of up to
. . . . (figures) . . . . (words) in the event that . . . . .fails to
fulfil the said contract, provided that your claim is received in writing at this office
accompanied by your signed statement that . . . . has failed to fulfil the contract.
Such claim shall be accepted as conclusive evidence that the amount claimed is due
to you under this guarantee.

For the purpose of identification, your request for payment must bear the confirmation
of your bankers that the signatories thereon are authorized so to sign.

This guarantee shall expire at close of banking hours at this office on . . . . and
any claim hereunder must be received at this office before expiry.

After expiry this guarantee shall become null and void whether returned to us for
cancellation or not. Any claim or statement received after expiry shall be ineffective.

This guarantee may not be transferred or assigned and shall be governed by
. . . . law; place of jurisdiction is . . . .

Figure 5.3   Specimen performance bond

strain on many customer/bank relationships when the customer has attempted to prevent the bank from meeting a demand for payment from the beneficiary. Although the customer may insist that the demand for payment is unfair and that he has carried out his obligations, unless he can get an injunction from the courts to prevent the bank paying, it is bound to honour its bond.

So far as banks are concerned, their bonds, which are used across the world, must be seen to be free from any third party intervention, otherwise their value to traders will be lost.

Retention bonds

The **retention bond** is a regular feature of many international contracts where the work undertaken may not be fully accepted until sufficient time has passed for any faults or omissions to be detected. Machinery, for example, installed to produce door panels for cars needs to be tested for quality, speed of production and operational reliability before a buyer is prepared to pay the full contract price. The retention bond enables him to claim if the machinery fails to meet the contract requirements. It is usually for up to 15% of the contract value and gives the supplier the opportunity to obtain 100% payment for the contract for the cost of the bond. When interest rates are high this can make a valuable contribution to the supplier's liquidity as he can have the use of 15% cash for several months before a claim may be made.

Advance payment bonds

In large international contracts it is not unusual for the contractor or seller to ask for an advance payment to meet initial costs and possibly secure supplies from third parties. These advances are generally for a maximum of 20% of the contract amount and understandably the buyer wishes to ensure that he can get his advance back if the seller or contractor fails to carry out his obligations. He therefore asks his bank, who makes the advance, normally through an overseas correspondent, to obtain an advance payment guarantee from the beneficiary, issued by a bank acceptable to the buyer's bank (Fig. 5.4). The bond is often presented as a document required under a documentary credit and is generally reduced as and when the seller ships the goods. In this case, it is important to ensure that the bond expires at least 10 days after the documentary credit. Thus, if the beneficiary presents documents on the expiry date of the credit and the negotiating or issuing bank completes its examination, say, 3 days later and finds the documents are out of order, the bond will still be valid and any outstanding advance can be reclaimed.

We understand that you have concluded a contract No . . . . with . . . . on . . . . for the supply of . . . . at a price of . . . . According to the terms of the contract you will make an advance payment of . . . . to . . . . As security for the possible claim for the refund of the advance payment, in the event that contractual delivery obligations are not fulfilled, a bank guarantee shall be provided.

At the request of . . . . we, ... hereby irrevocably undertake to refund to you on your first demand, irrespective of the validity and the affect of the above mentioned contract and waiving all rights of objection and defence arising therefrom, the advance payment or such amount as remains unpaid.

. . . . (in words . . . .)

upon receipt of your duly signed request for payment stating that . . . . . have failed to fulfil their contractual delivery obligations.

The total amount of this guarantee will be reduced by any payment effected hereunder.

For the purpose of identification, your request for payment must bear the confirmation of your bankers that the signatories thereon are authorized so to sign.

The amount of this guarantee will automatically be reduced in proportion to the value of each part-shipment upon receipt of us of copies of the relevant documents which we shall be entitled to accept as conclusive evidence that such part-shipment has been effected.

This guarantee shall expire at close of banking hours at this office On . . . . (in words . . . .)

If your claim has not been made on or before that date, regardless of such date being a banking day or not, this guarantee shall become null and void whether returned to us for cancellation or not. Any claim or statement received after expiry shall be ineffective.

This guarantee shall come into force only after receipt by us of confirmation that the advance payment has been received by . . . .

This guarantee is governed by . . . . law, place of jurisdiction is . . . .

Figure 5.4   Specimen advance payment guarantee

Issuing guarantees

Banks are constantly issuing a wide range of guarantees connected with transactions involving their customers. The bank's customer requests the issue of a guarantee which may be required under a contract that he has entered into. The wording has to be agreed between bank and customer and any ambiguity removed to prevent unfair calling or misunderstanding. Once agreed, the bank prepares the guarantee for issue and simultaneously asks the customer to sign a counter-indemnity worded exactly the same as the guarantee. The reason for this is obvious: the bank assumes a risk immediately it issues its guarantee and must ensure that if it is called, the counter-indemnity will enable it to claim on the customer for the amount of the call. When a guarantee is issued, it creates a series of contracts between the parties as shown in Table 5.1. It is entirely independent of the underlying commercial contract and should not contain details of that contract except by way of some identification to link the two.

Table 5.1

Parties to a guarantee	*Contractual relationship*
Principal (debtor)	Principal – beneficiary
Guarantor bank	Principal – guarantor bank
Correspondent bank	Guarantor bank – correspondent bank
Beneficiary	Guarantor bank – beneficiary

Where the correspondent bank issues its own guarantee rather than pass on the guarantee of the issuing bank, a further contract between it and the beneficiary is created as shown in Figures 5.5 and 5.6.

Conditional guarantees

Banks rarely issue this type of guarantee, which requires compliance with a condition generally made in the form of a supporting document. The introduction of conditions immediately exposes the bank to possible dispute with its customer or, worse still, involvement in a dispute between

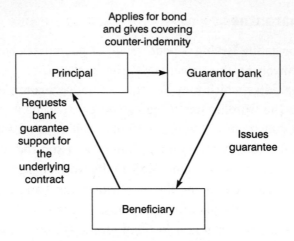

Figure 5.5

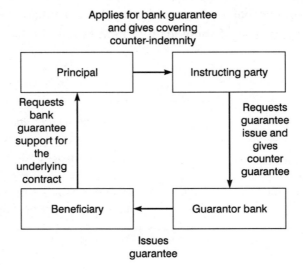

Figure 5.6

customer and beneficiary. The on-demand guarantee should require no proof that the beneficiary's claim is valid and honestly made. Occasionally, however, the principal insists that any claim under a guarantee which he wishes his bank to issue is accompanied by a document or documents proving breach of contract or default. The type of document called for to meet the guarantee's requirements would normally be issued by a third party; an inspectors report is a good example. Although banks strongly resist the inclusion of documentary proof as a condition of payment under their guarantees, when they are obliged to submit to the demands of an important customer, they accept no responsibility for the veracity of supporting documents, which should always be issued by reputable third-party operators, such as superintending or inspection companies.

Expiry date

It is essential for an issuing bank to ensure that the principal and the beneficiary are in complete agreement with the stated expiry date. Moreover, if the guarantee is to expire abroad with a branch of the issuing bank or with its correspondent, the principal must be made aware of any local legal requirements which may vary the effective expiry date. This is particularly important when addressing guarantees to certain Middle East countries where they can be considered valid for up to one month beyond the stated expiry date. In such cases, and in accordance with local law, it is only necessary for the beneficiary to declare that his claim relates to events occurring before the original expiry date for the claim to be considered valid.

Making a demand

The beneficiary of a guarantee must make any claim strictly in accordance with the requirements set out. A demand which varies with the terms of a guarantee will almost certainly not be met by the guarantor. It is important to remember the contractual relationships set up when a guarantee is issued, as each of those relationships relies on documents which should be identical throughout. Quite simply, the guarantor bank takes a counter-indemnity from the principal, worded exactly in accordance with the guarantee it has issued. Likewise the overseas correspondent, when advising the guarantee, or issuing its own guarantee, relies on the original guarantor's instrument. Any deviation by the beneficiary from the precise terms of demand, if not detected by the correspondent bank, may mean that if it honours a claim it cannot obtain reimbursement from the guarantor. To demonstrate this absolutely critical risk in handling guarantees it is necessary only to study the ruling in an important legal case, I.E. Contractors Limited v. Lloyds Bank Plc and Rafidain Bank, 1990.

Rafidain Bank issued three guarantees on the instructions of Lloyds Bank and relied on the counter-guarantees given by Lloyds. The beneficiary made demands under all three guarantees and they were considered by the judge to be valid. When examining the Lloyds Bank counter-guarantees it was found that the wording for demands under one of them was very slightly different from the other two. The judge ruled that the Rafidain Bank claims against two counter-guarantees were valid but that under the third counter-guarantee their claim for reimbursement was dismissed.

And the difference in the wordings? Two guarantees were for 'any sum or sums which you may be obliged to pay under the terms of your guarantee'. The third was for 'any amount *you state* you are obliged to pay under the terms of your guarantee'. This was a very important case and demonstrated the need for absolute accuracy in wording claims under guarantees.

Pay or extend demands

It is quite common for banks to receive claims from beneficiaries worded in such a manner as to give the guarantor no option but to pay the claim or extend the validity. Obviously the guarantor will always extend to protect its customer. In many cases, the beneficiary has genuinely run out of time to complete his contractual obligations and realises that if he allows the guarantee to lapse it may not be renewed. It may be that there is actual default by the principal but the beneficiary wishes to give him time to remedy it, provided that the guarantee can be extended for a suitable period. The danger of this practice lies in the opportunity it affords the beneficiary to extend the time in which the contract should have been completed. It is difficult for the guarantor bank, which may find itself in the middle of a dispute between principal and beneficiary. Because of the very nature of bank guarantees and the reliance placed upon them by operators throughout the world, they must be seen to be completely independent of any contractual negotiations between the other parties.

Unfair calling

Unfair calling of guarantees has given rise to a series of legal cases where the principals have challenged claims made by beneficiaries on the grounds that their contractual obligations had been fully met. Guarantor banks do not have the right to refuse to honour their commitments, so their first aim, when receiving a call, must be to acknowledge the claim and arrange payment. In advising the principal the bank simply states that it is honouring the claim and requests reimbursement. It cannot form an opinion on the honesty of the demand as it is unaware of the underlying contract requirements and, indeed, it must not become involved in any investigation if the principal should challenge the demand. The only exception to this practice is where the issuing bank has notice of fraud and can offer solid proof of it. Such evidence must be absolutely conclusive and strong enough to submit to a court; it is not difficult to understand that banks are extremely reluctant to take legal action in respect of guarantees or to be drawn into an action between principal and beneficiary. For the courts to give any consideration to an application for an injunction preventing payment under a guarantee, the material evidence submitted must be such that the only realistic inference is that there has been fraud on the part of the beneficiary.

In United Trading SA v. Allied Arab Bank Limited (1985) it was stated that: 'the evidence of fraud must be clear, both as to the fact of fraud and as to the bank's knowledge. The mere assertion or allegation of fraud would not be sufficient'.

Governing law

It is essential for a guarantee to stipulate the applicable law to be observed in the event of legal action. The principal and beneficiary will both attempt to have the guarantee subject to the law of their own country, but the issuing bank must take a firm stand on this point and apply Article 29 of Uniform Rules for Demand Guarantees which states that the governing law should be that of the place of business of the guarantor or instructing party. The reasoning behind this is simple: it is extremely difficult to contest a claim in a foreign court due to differences in legal systems and language problems.

Mention has to be made of the practice in some countries of allowing a guarantee to be operative after the stated date of expiry. This can be dangerous for a bank which has allowed its guarantee to be governed by the laws of the beneficiary's country because it may hold a counter-indemnity from its principal which could only be actioned in the country of issue. The reader will recognize the risks arising from the two documents having legally recognized but different expiry dates.

Issuing and operating guarantees

There is no other instrument used in international trade finance which requires as much care and supervision as the on-demand guarantee (see Fig. 5.7). The reader will understand that the operation of an on-demand guarantee involves a string of undertakings and counter-undertakings. Thus, the counter-indemnity given by the principal to the issuing bank must be identical in every way to the guarantee which that bank issues. In turn, that guarantee supports the guarantee issued by the correspondent bank; for the correspondent bank to be able to obtain reimbursement for any claim it honours, the two instruments must be identical: I.E. Contractors v. Lloyds Bank and Rafidain Bank demonstrated the seriousness of even a minor difference in wording. The issuing bank therefore must observe a number of points in order to prevent future disputes. It must ensure that the way in which a guarantee can be called is totally unambiguous. If the guarantee is issued through a foreign correspondent that bank may do one of two things; it may authenticate and pass on the issuing bank's original guarantee, or it may issue its own guarantee. In the latter case the correspondent bank's guarantee will be in the local language. In whatever language a guarantee is re-issued, the issuing bank must ask for a copy in order to determine whether it agrees fully with the counter-guarantee given to the correspondent. If the issuing bank considers that the terms of the correspondent's guarantee differ from the original guarantee it must advise the correspondent immediately that, until the two guarantees are rendered identical, no claim from the correspondent bank could be accepted. This is because the issuing bank is relying on a counter-indemnity from the principal which is also different from the correspondent bank's guarantee. The principal must then be advised and asked whether he has any objections to the points of difference. If he does not, the issuing bank asks him for an amended form of counter-indemnity and amends its own original guarantee under advice to the correspondent. Upon expiry of its

Siporex Trade SA v. Banque Indosuez

This was a case in which the writer was personally involved and which demonstrated the intention of the courts that on-demand guarantees, if they were to maintain international respect, must be honoured where claims are worded fully in accordance with the requirements of the instrument; any underlying dispute between the buyers and sellers was deemed to be of no concern to the bank.

Background

At the request of its customer Comdel, Banque Indosuez, London issued a guarantee, the key words of which were:

'We hereby undertake to pay on your first written demand any sum or sums not exceeding US$1 982 000 in the event that, by latest 7 December 1984, no banker's irrevocable letter of credit has been issued in favour of Siporex SA by order of Comdel Ltd. Any claims hereunder must be supported by your declaration to that effect.'

Banque Indosuez subsequently issued the required irrevocable credit in favour of Siporex and advised it to them through Banque Indosuez, Geneva.

However, shortly after the credit was advised, Banque Indosuez, London received a claim from Siporex for the full amount payable under the guarantee. The very existence of the required credit prompted Comdel to insist on rejection of the Siporex claim, resulting in the action going to court.

In the court hearing, judgement was given for Siporex, the judge commenting that he was bound by authority to construe the guarantee as *unconditional*, payable on demand, *without reference to the underlying events*.

From the banking point of view, the decision was correct as the courts had so often stressed that the commercial world perceived on-demand guarantees as the mainstay of many transactions and as such, there could be no question of a bank not meeting its obligations under one; to do so would destroy the reliability of the instrument.

However, although banks always insist on honouring properly worded claims under their on-demand guarantees, they are often put under considerable pressure by their customer, principal of the guarantee, claiming 'unfair calling'.

The only way a bank can be prevented from paying a claim under an on-demand guarantee is if its customer is able to obtain a court injunction forbidding payment. Such injunctions are very rare, as the courts are concerned to demonstrate the importance of maintaining international faith in this instrument.

Comdel were, understandably, incensed at having to meet their counter-indemnity given to Banque Indosuez when, as they claimed, the very action covered by the guarantee, namely the issue of an irrevocable credit, had been completed.

It transpired that the terms of the issued credit were at variance with the underlying contract between Comdel and Siporex and the inference was made that as such, it was therefore not the required credit. The inference was unfortunate as the guarantee was payable if *no* irrevocable credit was issued; it did not state that it was required to be issued *exactly as* requested by Siporex.

The case is a classic example of why a bank which issues an on-demand guarantee will always honour any claim which complies with its terms, irrespective of any attempt by its customer to claim unfair calling.

Comdel were eventually able to recoup the amount paid after taking their case to the Court of Appeal and then to Arbitration.

Figure 5.7 Case study: on-demand guarantees

guarantee, the issuing bank must ask for its return from the correspondent and, until it is returned or some undisputed proof provided of its cancellation, the full risk against the principal must remain on the bank's records.

Although it is not always easy to obtain the return of any original guarantee, opportunities often arise which can assist. For example, where a performance bond is issued to replace a bid bond, it can include the following clause: 'This bond will only become operative upon the return to us for cancellation of our bid bond number . . . . for . . . . dated . . . . '

Uniform Rules for Demand Guarantees (Publication no. 458)

The guarantee is a relatively simple instrument and consequently the ICC rules governing its use are uncomplicated. Article 3 sets out the principal details required in a guarantee and emphasizes the need to avoid excessive detail. The guarantee should stipulate:

- the principal
- the beneficiary
- the guarantor
- the underlying transaction
- the maximum amount payable and currency in which it is payable
- the expiry date or expiry event
- the terms for demanding payment
- any provision for reduction of the guarantee amount.

Article 4

The beneficiary's right to make a demand is not assignable.

Article 5

All guarantees are **irrevocable** unless otherwise indicated.

Article 9

The guarantor will examine all documents presented to ascertain whether or not they conform to the terms of the guarantee (as in documentary credits, this means that the guarantor is not responsible for the veracity of any document).

Article 19

All documents including the demand must be presented to the guarantor before the expiry date. (Obviously, where a guarantee is domiciled with a correspondent bank, it may expire with that bank.)

Article 20

All demands must be made in writing including authenticated tele-transmissions or tested electronic data interchange (EDI) messages.

Article 24

Retention of the guarantee after expiry by the beneficiary does not preserve any rights under it. (But, as stated previously, every effort must be made to obtain return of the guarantee after expiry.)

Indemnities

Hardly a day passes in a busy trade finance department without the bank being involved in the issue or taking of an indemnity. This instrument is used to permit a transaction to be completed despite the fact that minor irregularities exist. An indemnity differs from a guarantee in that there are only two parties to it, the indemnifier and the indemnified. The indemnifier, in essence, agrees to hold the indemnified party free from all consequences which may arise as a result of him carrying out the wishes of the indemnifier. A simple and most common example is the indemnity given to a shipping company in order for it to release goods without the production of a bill of lading. Quite clearly, a carrier is contractually engaged to deliver the goods it carries to the rightful holders of bills of lading and would not wish to improperly release goods unless it was suitably indemnified. Voyages nowadays are so fast that in many instances the vessels arrive at ports of destination before the bills of lading. A customer, requesting a bank to issue an indemnity, is required to complete a counter-indemnity in favour of the bank and to undertake to hand the missing document to the bank immediately it comes to hand. Banks treat indemnities as contingent liabilities and set them against the customer's facilities; they also insist on the return of all indemnities before taking them off risk. The presentation of irregular documents against documentary credits often necessitates the beneficiary obtaining from his bank an indemnity against which the negotiating bank is prepared to make payment. Even though his documents are out of order, a beneficiary may decide to obtain payment against an indemnity for four reasons.

1 He considers his buyer, the applicant for the credit, will waive the discrepancies.
2 He urgently needs payment in order to pay his supplier; the beneficiary is not always the actual supplier.
3 The payment may considerably reduce his bank borrowings and consequently the interest incurred.
4 The bank providing the indemnity may demand that payment by the negotiating bank is made direct to itself in order to reduce the beneficiary's borrowings or to release facilities for other transactions.

The cost to him is simply the commission his bank charges for the indemnity. It follows that banks exercise caution in the use of indemnities and only issue them for trustworthy customers.

Standby letters of credit

Sometimes described as a 'negative' letter of credit, the standby credit has assumed considerable importance in recent years with the growth of oil trading. It was developed in the early 1950s by American and Japanese banks in order to overcome the law in their countries which forbids banks from issuing guarantees; hence its negative characteristics. It is now used throughout the world and is subject to a set of rules introduced in 1998 by the ICC (International Standby Practices 98). Those rules proved necessary to remove the previous need for banks to issue standbys in accordance with UCP500 which, in many respects, was quite inappropriate. It differs considerably from the documentary credit as the following comparison shows:

- a **documentary letter of credit** undertakes payment when the beneficiary **carries out** his contract with the buyer
- a **standby letter** of credit undertakes payment when the applicant **fails to carry out** his contract with the beneficiary.

The credit is therefore similar in many respects to an 'on demand' guarantee; it is different in form but produces the same result. An important distinction between the standby credit and the documentary credit lies in the accepted feature of the latter, i.e. that documents presented generally represent security for the bank by providing title to goods. Under a standby credit the documents called for do not represent goods and are certainly not any form of security.

What are standby credits used for?

1 In support of construction contracts where default or improper performance by the contractor would be financially detrimental to the buyer. Thus the contractor would be penalized by any claim under the standby and its existence becomes a strong incentive for him to correctly carry out his contractual obligations.
2 To cover reinsurance companies against failure by their insurers to reimburse them for claims settled within the terms of an agreement between the companies.
3 In cases where companies are purchasing oil in the market and the cargoes which are offered have already been bought and sold several times. Thus, the original bills of lading have been issued to a third party and require a number of endorsements before they can give title to the final buyer. A documentary credit is therefore of little use in this case and the standby credit enables the beneficiary to receive payment without having to present the relative bills of lading and possibly other important documents.
4 To reduce the cost of providing a continuous stream of documentary credits covering trade between a buyer and an overseas supplier.

The following example illustrates this latter procedure.

Universal Power Stations Ltd (UPS) in Hull, United Kingdom wish to enter into a contract to purchase 600 000 metric tons of coking coal from Australian Open Mines Ltd (AOM), Darwin at the rate of 50 000 metric tons per month from January, price US$95 per metric ton.

AOM ask for payment by irrevocable documentary credit, but to open one credit for 12 months' supply (US$57 000 000) would block UPS's bank facilities and would also be very costly.

A standby credit is particularly appropriate for this situation and can reduce the strain on UPS' facilities; the method operates as follows.

1 UPS enters into a contract with AOM by which AOM agrees to supply 50 000 metric tons of coal each month for 12 months **on open account**.
2 In return for AOM's agreement, UPS arranges for its bank to issue a standby credit in their favour for US$9 500 000, being the value of 2 months' supply.
3 AOM will ship 50 000 metric tons in January and invoice UCPS direct with a request for payment by 15 February; they will repeat this procedure each month for 12 months.
4 If, by the 15th of any month, UPS have failed to settle the AOM for the shipment made in the previous month, AOM simply submit a claim for the invoice amount under the standby credit.
5 The reason for the credit covering 2 months' shipments is to allow for the possibility of UPS not paying, say by 15 May for the April shipment while AOM may have made a further shipment between 1 May and 15 May. AOM are thus protected against UPS failing to pay for both April and May shipments.
6 Obviously, immediately AOM are obliged to use the standby credit, they would stop further shipments pending an explanation of UPS's default.

Because of its close similarity to an 'on-demand guarantee', the standby credit has become widely used to support a wide variety of financial undertakings.

Most standbys are actually **payable at the issuing bank's counters** even though they may be in favour of a foreign beneficiary and advised through a correspondent bank.

The correspondent may:

- simply advise the standby to the beneficiary; or
- advise and confirm the standby to the beneficiary; or
- issue its own standby using the original standby as its security.

The most important feature of the standby is the fact that it is payable on unsupported demand.

It therefore becomes a powerful weapon in the hands of the beneficiary and the applicant must be confident that it will not be misused. If that confidence is weak, the applicant may ask for documentation to be presented to support any claim made against a standby credit; for example a surveyor's report, a copy bill of lading or an alleged unpaid invoice.

The applicant has to understand and accept that banks handling standbys which call for additional documents by way of proof that the beneficiary's claim is valid, will only verify that such documents are drawn up as required and not that what they purport to prove is true.

International Standby Practices: ISP98

The essential differences between standby credits and documentary credits are obvious to those who regularly deal in them, but ISP98 has introduced rules which emphasize that the differences are much greater than appear at first glance.

Let us look at the principal articles of ISP98 which set the standby in a class of its own.

Article 1.06(a)

All standbys are automatically **irrevocable**.

Article 1.06(e)

Any amendment once advised by an issuing bank cannot be revoked, even though the applicant may not have authorized such amendment.

Article 1.11(c)

The issuing and confirming banks are treated as separate issuers. The beneficiary of a transferred standby is known as the transferee beneficiary.

Article 2.01(b)

A standby may be available
(i)   at sight
(ii)   by acceptance
(iii) by deferred payment
(iv)   by negotiation.

Article 2.03

This is an important article. A standby is considered as issued when it leaves the issuing bank unless it clearly specifies that it is not then 'issued' or 'enforceable'. Applicants should be careful to use the protection of this clause if necessary and beneficiaries must watch for the inclusion of any statement which could render a standby useless.

Article 2.06(a)

A standby may state that it is subject to automatic amendment and such amendments are effective without consent.

Article 3.07(a)

Failure to make any one presentation out of a number of scheduled or permitted presentations does not prejudice the beneficiary's right to make further presentations. This is the direct opposite of UCP500 (Article 41) relating to shipment by instalments.

Article 3.09

The beneficiary's request to extend the expiry date must be treated as a demand for payment or a consent to the amendment.

Article 3.10

This article is incredible! The issuer is not required to notify the applicant of a presentation under the standby. Best ignored!!

Article 3.14(a)

If the place for presentation is closed on the last business day for presentation, then the last day for presentation is automatically extended to the day occurring **thirty calendar days after the place for presentation reopens for business.**

Article 4.10

No standby credit should contain a document to be issued by or countersigned by the applicant.

Article 4.13(a)

A bank honouring a presentation is not obliged to ascertain the identity of the person making the presentation. (Issuing banks should ask applicants whether they wish to omit this article.)

Article 4.16(a)

A demand for payment need not be separate from the beneficiary's statement or other required document.

Article 4.16(b)

If a separate document is required, it must contain:
(i)   a demand for payment from the beneficiary directed to the issuer or nominated person

(ii)   a date indicating when the demand was issued

(iii) the amount demanded

(iv)   the beneficiary's signature.

Article 5.01

Notice of dishonour must be given within a time after presentation of documents which is not unreasonable. Notice given within 3 business days is deemed to be not unreasonable and beyond 7 days is deemed to be unreasonable. (A prudent and conscientious banker would be well advised not to exceed the 3 days.)

Article 6.02

A standby is not transferable unless it so states. If it is stated to be transferable **it may be transferred in its entirety more than once (unlike the documentary credit) but it may not be partially transferred**. It cannot be transferred without the consent of the issuer, the nominated bank and the confirmer (if any).

Article 8.04

Any instruction or authorization to obtain reimbursement from another bank is subject to ICC Rules for Bank-to-Bank Reimbursement.

Gdanski Construct SA is a Polish construction company specializing in the fabrication and erection of single-span buildings; they have an excellent track record of installations in various European and Asian countries, including large aircraft hangars at three airports, several huge warehouses and a dry-dock complex.

They are preparing to bid at Can. $7 500 000 for the supply of a steel structure building in Toronto, for use as an indoor sports centre; the buyer in Toronto is a major leisure group, Combinex Inc. Their bid must be accompanied by a bid bond for 5% of the contract value; if they are successful that bid bond will be automatically converted into a 10% performance bond.

The terms of the tender will require the successful bidder to accept the following terms:

1 All materials for the construction are to be delivered within 4 months from the contract date.

2 Construction work is to commence within 5 months from the contract date and to be completed 9 months from the commencement date.

3 Terms of payment:

Materials
- 10% advance payment upon contract signing
- 80% upon shipment
- 10% on final completion of the building.

Construction
- 10% advance payment upon contract signing
- 30% by three stage payments – groundwork, steel framework, brickwork
- 10% upon completion of the building
- 10% upon acceptance of the building as evidenced by independent surveyor's report
- 40% by four promissory notes, each for 10%, payable at intervals of one year from the date of acceptance.

You are required to:

1 Identify the risks which Gdanski Construct SA face if they are awarded the contract.

2 Detail the bank products which you would advise them to demand from Combinex in order to reduce or eliminate those risks and to effect payments in accordance with the contract.

3 Identify the risks which Combinex Inc. face once the contract has been awarded.

4 Detail the products which you advise them to demand from Gdanski in order to reduce or eliminate those risks and to achieve completion of the contract.

Figure 5.8 Case study

Chapter 6

Insurance

Short-term export credit insurance

Most large industrial countries have specialist institutions set up to provide exporters with insurance cover against a variety of risks encountered when dealing with overseas buyers. The large institutions in Europe, the United States and Japan are mainly government-controlled or are joint ventures between banks, insurance companies and governments. Obviously, these institutions share one main aim and that is to promote exports from their own countries while, at the same time, protecting exporters against:

- commercial risks
- sovereign risks
- exchange risks

Main features of UK cover

1 Cover is usually for a maximum of 6 months' credit period.
2 Limit of cover is 90% for buyer risk and 95% for sovereign risk.
3 The exporter must place all his exports with the insurer except where he is the beneficiary of an irrevocable credit.

Risks covered

1 Insolvency of buyer.
2 Failure by buyer to pay within 6 months of due date for goods which he has accepted.

3 Buyer's failure to take up the goods.

4 Any embargo by the government in the buyer's country that prevents the import of goods which the exporter has contracted to sell.

5 External debt moratorium declared by the buyer's government.

6 Cancellation of export licence/import licence.

7 Shortfall resulting from the settlement in local currency and subsequent conversion to foreign currency (delay risk).

8 War, strikes, riots, civil commotions.

9 Voyage diversion.

Export credit cover is related solely to financial risk, not to physical risks such as transit risks. However, in one particular instance (3), the seller is covered for any loss suffered in either recovering the goods or finding another buyer. But he pays the first 20% of the loss and the insurer pays only 90% of the balance.

Export credit insurance policies as security

Banks will obviously be greatly influenced in deciding on facilities for export customers by the fact that they have export credit insurance cover. Any form of export finance must take into account the quality of the sovereign risk and the security available to the bank and the creditworthiness of the buyer.

Therefore, if an exporter has export credit insurance on all his overseas buyers, his bank can immediately assess the maximum risk they are prepared to take on any one buyer and all the buyers collectively. This is because the insurers will have set their limits for that exporter on all those buyers who they are prepared to insure.

Although a bank may consider the insurers' financial information on the buyers as sufficiently accurate, they are strongly advised to obtain their own status reports and to update them regularly.

Security

Any export credit insurance policy may be assigned to an exporter's bank and will allow the bank to claim against the policy in its own right and to claim against any particular buyer. **However, it must not be assumed that assignment of the policy gives the bank complete protection**.

Why?

1 The exporter may have defaulted on the payment of the insurance premiums.
2 He may have breached his contract with the buyer (faulty goods, late delivery etc.).
3 The individual limit on the buyer may have been exceeded.

The lessons are obvious: banks must treat export credit insurance cover in the same way as open cover marine insurance and should:

- have the policy assigned to the bank
- have the premiums paid by standing order/direct debit, etc.
- regularly check on any variation in the nature of the exporter's trade
- ensure that all amendments to the policy are notified direct to the bank
- regularly obtain updated status reports on the buyers.

The bank should understand that there are closely observed conditions relating to the payment of claims under export credit insurance. Payment delays vary, depending on the nature of the claim and range from 1 month after resale of goods not accepted by the buyer to 6 months for payment default and 4 months for any other type of loss. Claims for insolvency of the buyer are generally paid without delay but the insured party must provide the insurers with the necessary proof. During the waiting period for any claim, the bank must exercise caution over any subsequent consignment to the overseas buyer involved in the claim in case the cover is temporarily or permanently withdrawn.

Export credit agencies provide a range of policies designed to meet most exporters' needs and at the same time allow them to exercise some choice where the insurer's conditions are unacceptable. The most commonly used is the comprehensive policy for exporters who are selling regularly to established customers. However, except when the exporter is the beneficiary of an irrevocable credit, in which case cover is not required, he has to agree to insure his whole export turnover with that insurer for up to 3 years. By agreeing, he becomes eligible for more favourable premiums. Endorsements can be made to the comprehensive policy when the exporter is selling to affiliate companies and subsidiaries overseas, where the commercial risks are not covered but the political risks are. In addition, when extended credit is demanded by the overseas buyer, the comprehensive policy can be endorsed to allow cover to run for up to 5 years. In overseas construction and service contracts, there is generally a requirement for the shipment of goods to support the construction work and although the main contract may run for 5 years or more, cover for those goods is provided by a constructional works policy.

Marine insurance

No international trade transaction involving the movement of goods can be effected without the goods being insured against the appropriate risks. The contract between buyer and seller determines which party is responsible for arranging insurance according to the terms of despatch. Most importers buy on FOB (free on board) or CFR (cost and freight) terms in order to save foreign exchange, although the exporter will want to be sure that his buyer has comprehensive insurance cover in case his goods are damaged or lost before the buyer settles his invoice. Sea, air, road and rail consignments are all subject to a variety of risks, depending sometimes on the nature of the goods being carried and including criminal action such as piracy. When banks are financing international transactions they are, understandably, concerned that they do not incur additional risk by failure on the part of the exporter or importer to effect adequate marine insurance. Consequently the importer's bank will verify the type of cover its customer has, the quality of the insurers, any excesses or restrictions and the maximum amount payable, before agreeing to provide finance.

The importer

When goods are purchased on an FOB or CFR basis, it is the responsibility of the buyer to effect insurance cover.

Most importers have open-cover marine insurance which allows them to insure any number of shipments in a given month and only declare them at the end of the month. This is known as 'lost or not lost' cover and permits buyers to claim for losses which may have occurred before the shipments were declared.

The buyer's bank will require its customers' insurers to note in their records that the bank has a financial interest in the policy and may make claims in its own name. To protect its interest, the bank must check the nature of the insurance cover, the full extent of risks covered and any restrictive clauses. Subsequently, it must regularly check that the cover has not been amended in any way which could disadvantage the bank, and that premiums are paid up-to-date.

When an exporter despatches goods to his buyer on FOB or CFR terms, he is normally required to advise the buyer telegraphically within 2 days of despatch, giving essential details of the consignment. For goods sent by sea, those details would include value and date of shipment, name of carrying vessel, number of packages or tonnage, etc. The importer can then make the necessary declaration to his insurers.

Although each party to a contract of sale knows who is responsible for effecting insurance, it is not uncommon for an exporter to declare shipments under his own open cover even though he is supplying on FOB or CFR terms. He does this because he may be uncertain of the buyer's cover terms and prefers to make certain that until his goods are actually on the carrying vessel, they are properly insured. Once on board, goods shipped FOB or CFR become the responsibility of the buyer. In certain situations an exporter may effect insurance on behalf of the buyer because he is able to negotiate better terms with his insurers. He still ships FOB or CFR and settles insurance charges separately.

The exporter

Any exporter selling goods on CIF (cost insurance and freight) or CIP (carriage and insurance paid) is responsible for effecting insurance on them. He must arrange cover against the risks or on the terms detailed in his contract with the buyer and submit an insurance certificate or policy to enable the buyer to claim should any loss be incurred. The insurance document details the type of cover provided, identifies the consignment and must be issued in a form which will enable it to be transferred by endorsement, thus permitting the buyer or his bank, if it is financing the transaction, to make a claim for any loss.

Marine risks

There are fundamental marine risks against which all goods in transit should be insured. Many importers and exporters, when detailing the risks they wish to have covered, simply stipulate 'all risks' – 'war, strikes, riots and civil commotions'.

In essence, cover against these risks is, for most goods, perfectly adequate Article **28** (UCP600) states 'where a credit requires insurance against "all risks" and an insurance documents is presented containing any "all risks" notation or clause, whether or not bearing the heading "all risks", the insurance document will be accepted without regard to any risks stated to be excluded. The reader will understand that for most manufactured and packed goods the all risks and war etc. cover described is sufficient. However, not all goods carried by sea, air, canal, rail or truck can be fully insured under general cover. They may have peculiarities which necessitate special storage, controlled temperatures and avoidance of contact with other cargo; consequently they require specific types of insurance'.

Institute Cargo Clauses

The most widely used marine insurance cover is provided by the Institute of London Underwriters which introduced a range of separate clauses designed to meet the needs of international operators, whether trading in manufactured goods, raw materials or commodities: they are known as Institute Cargo Clauses.

For general cargo all risks cover is provided by Institute Cargo Clauses A.

In addition, Institute Cargo Clauses B and Institute Cargo Clauses C are designed to protect goods from a range of intermediate risks (B clauses) and major casualties (C clauses).

Specific cover is provided for a variety of commodities, for example Institute Rubber Clauses, and Institute Coffee Clauses.

Most marine insurance should be effective from seller's warehouse to buyer's warehouse, although some warehouse-to-warehouse clauses limit the cover, after discharge at the port of destination, to 15 days for local warehouses and up to 60 days for inland warehouses.

Losses

Many operators find it difficult to understand how insurers assess losses under marine policies; there are four main categories.

Total loss

Loss of the whole shipment due to the occurrence of a risk insured against, for example fire, collision and heavy seas. Shippers would expect 100% payment for such a loss.

Total loss of part of shipment

This relates to shipments which comprise a number of packages or cases. When one or more of them is damaged or lost, the whole shipment is considered as lost.

General average loss

A marine loss which occurs when part of a cargo is damaged by fire, contact with water or is simply jettisoned on instructions of the ship's master as a measure of safety and to prevent further damage to other cargo and to the vessel. Those shippers whose goods have remained undamaged as a result of the carrier's action are considered under maritime law as liable to contribute to the losses of the less fortunate shippers.

Particular average loss

This is a loss suffered by a shipper whose goods are damaged or partly lost due to a risk insured against. Where this type of cover is in force, no loss falls on those shippers whose goods are undamaged.

Chapter 7

Foreign exchange risk

Exchange risk is present in all transactions between foreign countries and increases with the length of time taken to fulfil a contract. Exporters and importers can reduce and sometimes eliminate exchange risks by using certain techniques available with their banks. The aim of any operator must be to fix, as near as possible, the rate of exchange at which he will have to settle a transaction at a future date. Unfortunately it is never easy to accurately forecast when goods will be shipped and paid for and operators understandably require a degree of flexibility in the settlement period. A classic example of the need to fix exchange rates forward is demonstrated by the large mail order groups who have to prepare extensive catalogues which include foreign goods purchased many months in advance of actual sales. The prices quoted in the catalogues must be realistic to the buying public and can only be arrived at by using forward cover for their purchases.

There are three principal techniques designed to meet the requirements of international trade operators in covering exchange risks.

1 The fixed forward contract.
2 The option forward contract.
3 The foreign currency option.

To understand these products, it is necessary to be able to calculate fixed and option forward rates using the spot as a base and adjusting for the premium or discount.

What is a rate of exchange?

It is simply the price of one currency expressed in the terms of another currency.

Spot rate of exchange

A rate of exchange for a foreign currency transaction which is to be settled within 2 working days of agreeing the rate.

How is it quoted?

On 1 January the spot rate for US dollars was 1.4316–1.4324 against Sterling.

Banks always sell low and buy high which means they sell at 1.4316 and buy at 1.4324.

Forward premium and discount

Currencies quoted forward are subject either to a premium or a discount depending on whether they are appreciating or depreciating. For example, on 1 January the 3 month forward US Dollar against Sterling is at a premium of 0.80–0.64 cents and is therefore more expensive than the spot dollar. Consequently, a merchant purchasing US Dollars on 1 January for delivery on 31 March will receive less dollars than for a spot purchase.

Fixed forward exchange contracts

This is a rather inflexible method of arranging forward currency deals which is only attractive to exporters and importers who know the exact date on which the transaction is to be completed; a good example is the payee of an accepted bill of exchange. The bank has only to commit itself to completion on a specific date and therefore calculating the forward rate is quite simple.

Calculation

Spot rate on 1 January	1.4316–1.4324
3 months forward premium	0.80–0.64 cents

Selling

Spot rate	1.4316
Deduct 3 months premium	0.0080
3 months forward rate	1.4236

Buying

Spot rate	1.4324
Deduct 3 months premium	0.0064
3 months forward rate	1.4260

Option forward contracts

Even if an exporter or an importer is uncertain of the exact date on which he will have to settle a contract, he can still arrange forward cover. The option forward contract enables the customer to fix a rate of exchange but allows him to complete the transaction on any day during an option period. On 1 January he may be reasonably sure that he will need to buy or sell a currency during the period 1–31 March. By entering into an option forward contract he can complete on any date in that option period.

Calculations for dealing in US dollars 3 months forward on 1 January with option 1–31 March

Selling

Spot rate on 1 January	1.4316
Deduct 3 months premium	0.0080
3 months forward contract with	1.4236
option 1–31 March rate	(Bank uses 31 March rate)

Buying

Spot rate on 1 January	1.4324
Deduct 2 months premium	0.0050
3 months forward contract with	
option 1–31 March rate	1.4274
	(Bank uses 1 March rate)

If the two months forward dollar is at a discount of 0.34–0.42 and the three months forward dollar is at a *discount* of 0.50–0.64 to sterling on 1 January then the calculation is:

Selling

Spot rate on 1 January	1.4316
Add 2 months discount	0.0034
3 months forward contract with	1.4350
option 1–31 March rate	(Bank uses 1 March rate and *only adds 2 months discount*)

Buying

Spot rate on 1 January	1.4324
Add 3 months discount	0.0064
3 months forward contract with	1.4388
option 1–31 March rate	(Bank uses 31 March rate and *adds 3 months discount*)

Remember, banks sell low and buy high and will always use the rate for the option period which is in their favour.

Closing out forward contracts

When a customer enters into a forward contract with his bank to either purchase or sell a currency, he undertakes to deliver to the bank the equivalent in another currency on the maturity date.

For example, a purchase of US$150 000 against Sterling on 1 January for delivery on 31 March at the rate of 1.4260 would engage the customer in paying the bank the Sterling equivalent (£105 189.34) on 31 March. However, if the customer fails to deliver the Sterling on the due date, the bank is obliged to **close out** the contract. This means that it unwinds the deal, using the spot market rates on 31 March.

Example

Customer sells US$150 000 against Sterling on 1 January at 3 months forward fixed (31 March) at 1.4260.

	Sell	Buy
Spot rate on 1 January	1.4316–1.4324	
3 months forward rate	1.4236–1.4260	
Spot rate on 31 March	1.4225–1.4250	

On 31 March the bank sells

$150 000 spot at 1.4250 producing	£105 263.16
Proceeds of $150 000 at 1.4260	£105 189.34
Profit to customer	£73.82

If the spot rate on 31 March was 1.4300–1.4325 the bank would sell at 1.4300:

Proceeds of $150 000 at 3 months rate 1.4260	£105 189.34
$150 000 sold spot at 1.4300	£104 895.10
Loss to Customer	£314.24

Borrowing in currency

An exporter who does not wish to enter into a forward exchange contract can still cover his exchange risk by borrowing in foreign currency the amount he expects to receive from his buyer at a future date. He can then convert the amount borrowed back into his own currency and use the funds to improve his liquidity until eventual payment by his overseas buyer. At that point he can extinguish his currency loan by using his buyer's currency payment and settle any interest due.

Buying currency and holding on deposit

This is a useful procedure that can be employed by an importer to fix the rate of exchange at which he will have to meet a future currency commitment. He buys the amount of currency required at spot rate, places it on deposit and uses it to pay the foreign exporter in due course. Thus, at the time he purchases the currency he fixes his rate of exchange for a future payment.

Foreign currency options

Foreign currency options present the exporter or importer with an entirely different risk from spot and forward contracts, because an option is a **right**

to buy or sell but not a contractual obligation; they are called PUT options (sell) and CALL options (buy).

If we take the example used in fixed forward exchange contracts, an exporter, on 1 January, wishing to sell US dollars before 31 March, can buy a PUT option for an option premium (say 2% of deal value) at an agreed **strike price**.

Once he has paid the premium, he can:

1 exercise his option and sell the currency in March
2 abandon the option and lose his premium
3 sell back the option.

Let us assume that on 1 January for a premium of 2%, the exporter takes out an option to sell US$150 000 by 31 March at a **strike price** of 1.4236.

If, when the exporter receives the US dollars, the spot rate has **risen** by more than 2% (e.g. 1.4550) then, obviously, he will exercise his option at 1.4236.

Option
$150 000 @ 1.4236   £105 366.68
less 2% premium paid 'up front'   £2 107.33
                                                    £103 259.35

Spot sale
$150 000 @ 1.4550   £103 090.78
                                    (£166.57 **below** strike price
                             conversion, £103 259.35)
Profit to exporter =   £166.57

However, if the spot rate has **fallen** to 1.4150 the exporter would abandon his option and sell his US$ at spot.

$150 000 @ 1.4150   £106 007.07
less premium paid 'up front'   £2 107.33
                                                    £103 899.74
                                    (£640.39 **over** strike price
                             conversion, £103 259.35)
Profit to exporter =   £640.39

Chapter 8

Special types of credits

Since the documentary credit first appeared in trade finance almost 200 years ago, it has undergone many changes. Apart from its principal purpose of settling transactions between international merchants and traders, it has had to be adapted to meet changes in financial practice, modes of transport and the unification of international documentary credit practices.

A number of special types of credit have been developed which provide pre-shipment and post-shipment finance, enable buyers to regulate suppliers of essential raw materials and prevent over-stocking; in other words, they assist importers in exercising a discipline over their suppliers.

The transferable credit and its look-alike, the back-to-back credit, have given an opportunity to traders and middlemen to act as principals in markets to which, hitherto, they would have been denied access. Since 1962, Uniform Customs and Practice for Documentary Credits has been four times to meet many of these changes and to smooth the introduction of hybrid credits into day-to-day operations.

The revolving credit

This credit provides a means of controlling the frequency and value of goods which an exporter may ship to his buyer in a given period.

Manufacturers and merchants who require a limited amount of raw materials or commodities each month, for example in order to maintain production or to meet market requirements, are often reluctant to establish documentary credits for large amounts covering 6 of 12 months' purchases. But they need to regulate their suppliers' shipments and at the same time provide them with a guarantee of payment for a number of months or any other delivery periods. By using a revolving credit, a buyer can be certain that his supplier can only ship an agreed maximum quantity in any month, for example, but the supplier knows that when a shipment has been made, the credit will automatically revolve for another 6, 12 or however many months agreed between buyer and seller.

Example

A manufacturer of steel, using 5000 metric tons of iron ore per month might open a revolving credit of US$450 000 (5000 Mt @ $90 per Mt) and allow it to revolve six times at US$450 000 per month. This should ensure that each month the buyer receives the stipulated 5000 Mt and the seller cannot draw more than US$450 000 from the credit. Immediately one month's supply has been shipped, the credit becomes available for a further $450 000 the following month.

There are two types of revolving credits:

■ cumulative
■ non-cumulative.

The **cumulative revolving credit** allows the beneficiary to carry forward any balances not used in previous cycles. However, if we take the example of the steel manufacturer, we can see that a cumulative credit may be quite unsuitable for his requirements. If his bank opens a cumulative credit for US$450 000 to revolve over six periods of 1 month, the beneficiary may decide not to make any shipment during the first 5 months and then ship the whole 30 000 tons of iron ore in the sixth month, having accumulated US$2 250 000 over the 5 months. For the steel manufacturer this would be a quite unacceptable situation as he could exhaust his stock of iron ore and possibly have none for 3 or 4 months.

This demonstrates the weakness of the cumulative revolving credit; it can only operate satisfactorily when the seller acts in good faith and complies strictly with his contract terms.

The **non-cumulative revolving credit** does not allow any unused balances to be carried forward and would therefore be preferable for our steel manufacturer. The beneficiary would realize that if he did not ship 5000 tons in any particular month he would lose that portion of the credit.

So far as the issuing bank is concerned, when issuing a revolving credit, cumulative or non-cumulative, the risk on the importer is the aggregate value of all revolutions. If the value of 5000 tons of iron ore is $450 000, then a 6 month revolving credit is risked as $2 700 000 because that is the total value of iron ore that the beneficiary could ship over the full 6 months. Although revolving credits serve a useful purpose in regulating shipments, they lack any discipline to be exercised against the beneficiary. Even under a non-cumulative revolver he can delay shipping for any number of months and still know that he can ship on, say, months five and six and be paid. A better method of putting pressure on a supplier to adhere to an agreed shipping programme is for the importer to use an instalment credit.

Demonstration of commission saving

Goods:	6000 M tonnes steel @ US$190 M.T.C.I.F.
Shipment:	1500 M tonnes per month May/June/July/Aug 2003
Total value:	US$1 140 000
Opening commission:	¼% per 3 months

Example A

Straight L/C US$1 140 000 valid to 30.9.03 opened 1.3.03

¼% on US$1 140 000 × 3 quarters = $8 550

Example B

Revolving L/C for US$285 000 valid to 30.9.03 opened 1.3.03

Commission to 31.5.03 on $1 140 000 @ ¼% = $2850

Commission to 31.8.03 on $855 000 @ ¼% = $2137

Commission to 30.9.03 on $570 000 @ ¼% = $1425

Total $6412

Saving of $2138

Figure 8.1 Reducing commission by using a revolving letter of credit

The revolving credit can be less expensive to operate than a straight credit and applicants should ensure that the opening bank applies its commission, as shown in the example in Figure 8.1.

The instalment credit

This credit stipulates the exact amount that a beneficiary may use in a given period, say 1 month, and covers possibly 6 to 12 months. The beneficiary must ship the stipulated quantity of goods in each month, but immediately he fails to ship that amount in any one month the credit becomes invalid and can only be revalidated on the instruction of the importer. It is not difficult to see what sort of discipline this allows the importer to exercise over the beneficiary. Even worse for the latter, if he ships but presents discrepant documents, the credit is also invalidated. This type of credit is governed by Article 32 (UCP600) which will be discussed later in this chapter.

The red clause credit

This credit was originally designed for use in the Australian and New Zealand wool trade where exporters purchased their wool from a variety of small sheep farmers. It was a considerable hardship for those farmers to have to wait for payment until the exporter could draw against a documentary credit; in addition, there was always the risk to them that the exporter might fail to pay them at all. The pressure on exporters to meet the farmers' needs resulted in a special clause being inserted in documentary credits allowing the beneficiaries to draw advance payments for up to an agreed percentage of the credit amount. The clause was stamped on the original credit in red, hence its title. The advances were used to secure supplies of wool and accumulate them for baling and shipment. An essential feature of the red clause credit is that advances made are unsecured, and for that reason banks will only operate them for undoubted customers. They are an extension of a financial agreement between buyer and seller. So far as issuing and advising banks are concerned, the most important decision they have to make is in clearly establishing responsibility for the advances. Generally speaking, the issuing bank is liable to reimburse any advances made under an irrevocable credit, but advising banks that are unsure of this from the credit terms should refer back to the issuing bank before actually paying away funds.

The reader will understand that this type of credit presents the issuing and advising banks with risks not normally associated with documentary credits. In the first instance, the issuing bank is being asked to agree unsecured advances to a foreign beneficiary and runs the risks of non-repayment, or repayment and possible intervention by the beneficiary's central bank in refusing to release the foreign exchange. Unless the applicant is a very sound customer, the issuing bank may take a deposit equal to part or all of any red clause advances. It is easy to see, however, that the advising bank, requested to advance moneys under a foreign bank's credit, faces risks on the issuing bank and the beneficiary. Let us assume that a bank in France receives a red clause credit from a South American bank in favour of a wine exporter and that it permits advances for 20% of the credit amount which the bank makes against simple receipt. The receipt is worded to the effect that the beneficiary will refund all or part of the advance should he not ship the full quantity of goods within the validity of the credit. Failure by the beneficiary to refund leaves the advising bank with an unsecured risk on the issuing bank compared with a documentary risk when goods have actually been shipped, and where the documents represent a form of security.

Red clause credits offer the beneficiary more than simply an advance because the advising or confirming bank is secured by the undertaking given by the issuing bank in its irrevocable credit. As a consequence the advance should be made at a lower rate of interest than would normally be charged for direct borrowing by the beneficiary. The applicant is making a significant gesture in agreeing to the advance which the issuing bank will set against his credit lines. On this basis, it is not unreasonable that the applicant should seek some sort of price concession from the beneficiary. So far as the issuing bank is concerned, this is a direct and not a contingent liability, and therefore only accorded to first-class customers. Default by the beneficiary leaves the issuing bank with no merchandise as security. The reliability of the applicant cannot be too heavily stressed as it is not difficult to imagine how collusion between him and the beneficiary could defraud the bank. Additionally, the issuing bank should satisfy itself that the red clause advance meets a genuine commercial need and is not an attempt to fund an affiliated company at preferential rates. Understandably, advising banks are often reluctant to operate red clause credits because of the unsecured risk element. As an alternative, but more secure form of pre-shipment finance, the green clause credit is often preferred.

The green clause credit

This credit operates in the same way as the red clause except that all advances made to the beneficiary are against goods which must be warehoused in the bank's name. Control over those goods is entirely in the hands of the operating bank: it approves the warehouse, issues release notes whenever goods are required for shipment, has them consigned to the carrying vessel in the bank's name and ultimately takes title to them through the bills of lading. It is important that a bank operating a green clause credit follows each stage carefully to ensure that at no time does it lose title to the goods.

The advance payment credit

Although the red and green clause credits provide advance payments for the beneficiary, they may still be unacceptable to the issuing and advising banks from the point of security. It is possible that the beneficiary of a green clause credit does not deal in the type of goods which can be warehoused and controlled by the bank prior to shipment. He may be a manufacturer requiring the advance to convert machines in order to make a product which is intended specifically for one buyer. In this case, the issuing bank includes in its credit the requirement for the beneficiary to present a bank advance payment bond before the credit can operate and the advance can be made. He is paid the stipulated advance when the issuing bank has approved the bank providing the guarantee. It is important that the validity of the advance payment guarantee exceeds that of the credit by at least 14 days, preferably 1 month. This enables the advising or confirming and issuing banks to deal with any irregularities which may be found in the beneficiary's documents when they are presented for negotiation. The applicant may not agree to accept discrepant documents which were negotiated within the validity of the credit but which are referred to him 7

days afterwards. If the advance payment guarantee has expired simultaneously with the credit, a claim against it will not be honoured.

The transferable credit

International trade transactions regularly involve middlemen: traders who
buy from one supplier and simultaneously sell to another buyer. These
operators are skilled in the practice of locating products throughout the
world at competitive prices which enables them to sell on at a profit. In
many cases these middlemen do not have the financial muscle to buy on
their own account and require some assistance from their buyer. As an
answer to their problem the transferable credit is ideal (Fig. 8.2). A
transferable credit is simply an irrevocable documentary credit to which the
term 'transferable' has been added, allowing the beneficiary to transfer it to
a second beneficiary of his choice, known as the transferee. In essence, the
ultimate buyer, perhaps a Russian government department, enters into a
contract with a supplier in New York to purchase wheat. The New York
supplier has identified a source of wheat for which he has to pay by means
of an irrevocable documentary credit. In his contract with the Russian buyer
he will request settlement by a transferable credit which allows him to
transfer it to his own supplier. The transaction is now financed by two
credits, the original one from Russia and the transferred credit. UCP600
devotes an extended Article, 38, to the operation of transferable credits and
a close study of that Article will follow in this chapter. At this stage, it is
necessary only to mention the principal features of a transferable credit and
the details which may be altered when transfer is effected.

■ Unless a transferable credit permits part shipments, the amount can only
  be transferred **once**.
■ Where part shipments are permitted, partial transfers can also only be
  made **once**.
■ The beneficiary of the prime credit may be shown as the applicant for
  the transferred credit.
■ Alterations may be made to the amount, the price of the goods, latest
  shipment date, validity and insurance cover and number of days from
  date of transport document within which documents must be
  presented.

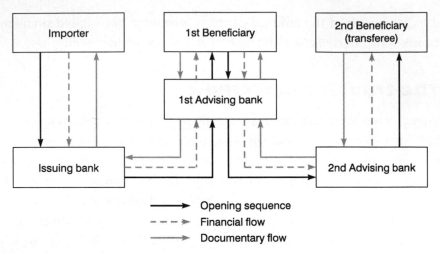

Figure 8.2 Transferable credit

At this point we will study the basic operation of this type of credit, the benefits it bestows on the middleman and the risks it presents to those banks involved in the operation chain.

At the outset an issuing bank is requested by its customer, the applicant, to establish a transferable credit in favour of his supplier. The bank may or may not agree depending on a number of factors, not least the risks involved. We have shown that in documentary credits, if the applicant fails to reimburse the issuing bank for a negotiation effected under credit, it still has control over the documents and ultimately over the goods when the vessel arrives. When issuing that credit the bank knows that the goods will be supplied by the beneficiary on whom, if it wishes, it can make enquiries as to track record and market reputation. With the transferable credit, however, the issuing bank does not know to whom the beneficiary may have it transferred; in many cases it is transferred to another country. The transferee, as the second beneficiary is known, may not ship goods of the quality required under the credit, so the original issuing bank has to be aware of the potential problems and endeavour to counter them as much as possible. When the transferable credit is issued, it is sent in the normal way to a correspondent advising bank for transmission to the beneficiary. It is identical to ordinary credits except for the simple addition of one word, transferable. The beneficiary will have found his ultimate supplier and returns to the advising bank with a request that the credit be transferred. At this point the advising bank has to decide whether it wishes to transfer the credit and incur the risks associated with it. Article 48 allows the beneficiary to request transfer but he has no right to demand it; the advising bank is also allowed to decline the request without necessarily giving the beneficiary a reason.

This situation is understandable if we follow the course of the credit assuming that the advising bank agrees to its transfer. The beneficiary of the transferable credit becomes the applicant for the transferred credit and gives a mandate to the advising bank, thus effectively acting as a customer. Clearly, any bank is entitled to choose who it wishes to have as customers and the mere fact that a middleman holds an irrevocable credit in his favour is not always sufficient to convince a bank to accept instructions from him. But let us assume that the beneficiary is of good standing and the advising bank agrees the transfer. It now issues a new credit in favour of the transferee and despatches it to a correspondent advising bank. The new credit is identical to the original credit so far as documentation is concerned but may vary from it on specific points. The first beneficiary expects to make a profit on the transaction, so the price of the goods and the credit amount are reduced. Article 48 permits a number of details which may be altered in the transfer, namely amount, price, expiry date, latest date for presentation of documents, the period for shipment and the percentage for which insurance may be increased under CIF credits. A new credit is now in force, available with a new correspondent advising bank which will handle it as a normal documentary credit; in many cases there is no indication that it is a transferred credit. Ultimately that bank negotiates documents presented by the transferee and sends them to the first advising bank. That bank examines them, decides whether they are in order or not and asks the first beneficiary to hand them his invoice addressed to the ultimate buyer, the applicant of the original credit. It then negotiates the documents against the original credit, reimburses its correspondent for its negotiation under the transferred credit and pays the middleman the difference between the two negotiations, which is his profit. This all sounds relatively straightforward and simple, so why do banks decline to get involved?

The greatest risk when handling transferable credits falls on the first advising bank and it is a technical risk: the possibility that it may honour a negotiation under the transferred credit, check the documents against the original credit and fail to detect a discrepancy for which the issuing bank refuses to pay. Additionally, the advising bank when issuing the transferred credit may make a mistake in transcribing the terms; remember the two credits are supposed to be identical. Finally, the bank effecting the transfer selects its correspondent with whom it has excellent working relations. Invariably transactions between two such banks will create problems, through discrepancies in documents for example, but under normal circumstances the issuing bank endeavours to have discrepancies waived by its customer, the applicant. With a transferred credit it has no option but to refuse any form of discrepancy because the middleman as applicant is not in a position to accept them; reference must be made all the way back to the bank which issued the original transferable credit. The possible damage to the relationship with the correspondent may not be considered as worth risking. The transferred credit must be considered as entirely separate from the original and therefore the transferring bank can only pay on complying documents presented by its correspondent. Whatever reimbursement arrangements are available in the master credit, the transferring bank must not allow telegraphic reimbursement in the transferred credit. The reason is simple: the bank nominated to advise the transferred credit could reimburse itself for a negotiation which is subsequently found by the first advising bank to be out of order. That bank would then be unable to obtain reimbursement under the master credit. The best course for a bank transferring a credit is to stipulate that it will reimburse the negotiating bank upon receipt of documents in order. It is not uncommon to see a clause in transferred credits stating that under no circumstances will discrepant documents be accepted.

As the transferable credit operates exactly as an ordinary documentary credit it can be available at sight, usance or by deferred payment. Serious complications can arise for the transferring bank if a credit which has been transferred to more than one transferee is amended as to availability, or vice versa. The possibility that the transferees will not all be in agreement is probably sufficient incentive for the transferring bank to refuse to agree to the amendment to the original credit, but it can only take that action if it has added its confirmation.

The beneficiary of the original credit is required to provide his invoice to the transferring bank when it receives documents under the transferred credit. In the event that he is unavailable or for any reason cannot present this invoice, the transferring bank is allowed to submit to the issuing bank those documents negotiated under the transferred credit. Much is written about the need to show the first beneficiary as the applicant of the transferred credit on the grounds that, if the transferee learns the name of the original applicant, he will make arrangements to deal with him direct and cut out the middleman. But the role of these middlemen is so important to the ultimate buyers, because of their access to a wide range of suppliers, that they have no fear of being usurped. It might take a buyer many days to find a suitable supplier whereas the middleman may do it in a matter of hours. The obvious risk of price movement is sufficient to show the exporter the value of using a middleman.

The back-to-back credit

Although a middleman may request his buyer to establish a transferable credit in his favour to enable him to pay his supplier, he knows there is no guarantee that the buyer's bank will agree to it. As an alternative when he receives an irrevocable documentary credit which is not transferable, he may try to persuade the advising bank to open a back-to-back credit (Fig. 8.3). He is seeking to do precisely what a transferred credit does, but for a variety of reasons he may find the advising bank unwilling to agree to his request. The back-to-back credit is simply the issue of one credit secured by another, referred to as the master credit. Upon receipt of a credit from his buyer, the beneficiary asks the advising bank to issue an identical credit showing himself as the applicant, in favour of his supplier. If the advising bank agrees, a new credit is issued, identical to the master credit with minor amendments to price, amount, validity and possibly insurance. Back-to-back credits are extremely risky for banks to undertake. No mention is made of them in UCP600, so to that extent they operate outside recognized practice. For that reason, any bank asked to open a back-to-back credit assesses the strength of the bank issuing the master credit and proceeds

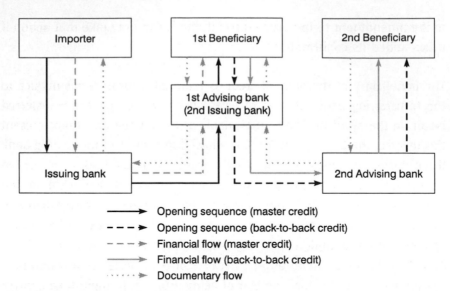

Figure 8.3   Back-to-back credit

only if it considers the middleman as reliable and competent to carry out his contract. By taking a pledge from the middleman for any rights he has under the original credit, the bank effectively establishes security for the back-to-back credit. It must be understood that by agreeing to issue this type of credit banks are making considerable concession to the applicants, and consequently apply very stringent risks as to their operation. Firstly, the applicant should be a customer of the bank or, if not, a potential customer whose business is attractive to the bank. Secondly, the bank should strongly resist any attempt by the applicant to allow the terms of the new credit to in any way vary from those of the master credit. The reason for that is simple: this is not a transferred credit: the ultimate buyer under the master credit is completely unaware that a back-to-back credit has been opened. Therefore if the documents presented under the back-to-back credit cannot be applied to the master credit, then the bank which issued the back-to-back creditmay fail to obtain reimbursement but will be obliged to honour its own credit. The master credit and the back-to-back credit must be identical and must be operated in tandem, and if amended must be subject to agreement by both beneficiaries. Ideally, no bank should agree to open a back-to-back credit unless it is the advising or confirming bank of the master credit, and if it is only the advising bank it should immediately confirm the master credit and advise the issuing bank. Its charges will be for account of the beneficiary. The reason is obvious: if the bank is to be solely liable to the beneficiary of the back-to-back credit it is assuming the role of an issuing bank and is depending upon the master credit for reimbursement of any payment it has to make under its own credit. Furthermore, as confirming bank, it has the right to accept or reject any amendment to the master credit if it wishes to protect its position under the back-to-back credit.

Back-to-back credits are in regular use and, if properly controlled, provide a means of finance for the middleman which he could not otherwise obtain.

How does the credit work?

Importer A in Turkey is purchasing 4000 metric tons of sugar from Merchant B in London and instructs his bank to open an irrevocable credit as follows:

Applicant	Importer A, Istanbul
Beneficiary	Merchant B, London
Amount	US$500 000
Expiry	30.9.03 in London
Goods	4000 metric tons of sugar @ US$124 per Mt

Merchant B is buying the sugar from Supplier C in Dominica, who demands payment by irrevocable documentary credit, but Merchant B either does not have the necessary banking facilities to open such a credit, or his own facilities are fully used. He therefore asks the London advising bank from whom he received the Turkish credit, or possibly his own bank, whether it is prepared to open a back-to-back credit in favour of his supplier in Dominica.

If the London bank agrees, the back-to-back credit would look something like this:

Applicant	Merchant B, London
Beneficiary	Supplier C in Dominica
Amount	US$480 000
Expiry	10.9.03
Goods	4000 metric tons of sugar @ US$120 per Mt

The reader will observe that in the back-to-back credit the validity has been shortened to 10 September 2003, i.e. 20 days before expiry of the master credit; this is done to prevent documents from Dominica arriving in London after 30.09.03, which would make them discrepant. Once both credits are in force, they operate in a manner similar to transferable credits.

Supplier C ships the sugar and presents his documents to the advising bank in Dominica which negotiates them, if in order, and forwards them to the issuing bank in London. That bank reimburses the Dominican bank and then applies the same documents (plus Merchant B's invoice which is substituted for Supplier C's invoice) against the master credit opened by Importer A. The London issuing bank sends the documents to the original issuing bank in Turkey and reimburses itself under the prime credit. The difference between the amount paid to Supplier C and the amount reimbursed under the master credit is paid to Merchant B and represents his profit.

The risks involved in opening back-to-back credits are obvious. The master credit could be amended with the first beneficiary's agreement in such a way that documents under the back-to-back credit would no longer be identical. For example, he could accept an amendment changing the quality of the goods from class B to class A. Unless the beneficiary of the back-to-back credit agreed to an identical amendment, the documents paid under that credit could not be tendered against the master credit. The bank opening the back-to-back credit may make an error in transcribing the terms from the master credit or in examining the documents under the back-to-back credit. In both cases the bank faces refusal by the original issuing bank for irregular documents. To avoid the difficulties which may arise if the master credit is amended, the advising or nominated bank should confirm it and advise the issuing bank. Then, as confirming bank, it has the right to accept or reject any amendment and protect its position under the back-to-back credit.

Any bank contemplating opening a back-to-back credit should take the following precautions.

If the beneficiary of the master credit is not a customer of the bank then they should obtain full status reports on the company before proceeding and must obtain and hold the original copy of the master credit. If they are not the advising bank for the master credit, they must obtain from the beneficiary a signed instruction to the advising bank that all amendments and correspondence must be sent direct to themselves and not to the beneficiary. At that point the beneficiary must be asked to obtain from the advising bank copies of any previous amendments. They must shorten the validity (and possibly the latest shipment date) of the back-to-back credit in order to ensure that documents negotiated under that credit can be presented within the validity of the prime credit. They should obtain, in advance, signed invoices from the beneficiary of the prime credit to be substituted for the invoices eventually presented against the back-to-back credit. Such invoices should be complete with the exception of date, quantity of goods and total value of shipment. Thus, if the first beneficiary is unable for any reason to present substituted invoices, the bank can still present a full set of documents to the bank which issued the master credit. A status report on the ultimate supplier is essential and the bank should endeavour to obtain from the first beneficiary some form of additional security (cash margin), rather then rely solely on the master credit.

A transferable credit which does not prohibit part shipments or drawings may be transferred to more than one transferee. For back-to-back credits, however, this raises a number of risks which advising or confirming banks are generally not prepared to accept; the technical risks alone are sufficient to deter most operating banks.

The main differences between a transferred credit and a back-to-back credit are:

1 When a transferable credit is transferred, it is done with the knowledge and consent of the issuing bank.
2 The issuing bank is unaware of the opening of a back-to-back credit; to that extent it is totally independent of the master credit.
3 When the bank which has effected the transfer of a credit eventually receives documents raised by the transferee and presented by its appointed advising bank, it immediately approaches the first beneficiary for his invoice. That invoice is then substituted for that of the transferee and together with the remaining documents is delivered to the issuing

bank. However, if the bank is unable to obtain the first beneficiary's invoice, Article 38 allows it to deliver to the issuing bank **those documents received under the transferred credit**.

With the back-to-back credit, if the advising bank is unable to obtain the first beneficiary's invoice, it is left with discrepant documents and has no option but to seek the issuing bank's acceptance of them. Hence there is no need with transferable credits to obtain invoices in advance for substitution, whereas with back-to-back credits such a precaution is essential.

UCP600

Instalment credits

Article 32 states that if drawings and/or shipments by instalments within given periods are stipulated in the credit and any instalment is not drawn and/or shipped within the period allowed for that instalment, the credit ceases to be available for that and any subsequent instalments unless otherwise stipulated in the credit.

The reader should understand that presentation of discrepant documents for an instalment also results in cancellation of any remaining instalments if the applicant refuses to waive the discrepancies, i.e. presentation of discrepant documents is, effectively, a **non-presentation**.

Transferable credits

Article 38 states, inter alia:

1 A credit may only be transferred by the bank authorized to pay, incur a deferred payment undertaking, accept or negotiate; if the credit is freely negotiable it can only be transferred by the bank specifically authorized to do so.

   Note: an exporter requesting his buyer to provide him with a transferable credit must understand that it may be advised through a bank which is unwilling to transfer it. If he elicits from his own bank in advance that it would be prepared to effect the transfer, he can ask his buyer to name it in the credit application as the preferred advising bank. It is worth a try and if successful can save the beneficiary a lot of time.

2 At the time of transfer the first beneficiary must irrevocably instruct the transferring bank as to whether he wishes to retain the right to refuse to allow the transferring bank to advise amendments direct to the second beneficiary (transferee) or allow them to do so.

3 If a credit is transferred to more than one second beneficiary, refusal of an amendment by one or more second beneficiaries does not invalidate the acceptance by the other second beneficiaries.

   Note: this is a difficult situation for advising or confirming banks, who may find themselves operating two completely different credits: one for the accepting beneficiaries and another for those who refused amendments. This is another example of why banks often decline to operate transferable credits.

4 The first beneficiary may request that payment or negotiation be effected to the second beneficiary at the place to which the credit has been transferred, up to and including the expiry date of the original credit unless that credit expressly states that it may not be made available for payment or negotiation at a place other than that stipulated.

Note: most advising banks insist that the transferred credit must expire at least 7–10 days before the original credit. This is the only way they can hope to have irregular documents corrected within the validity of the original credit.

General

Although transferable and back-to-back credits are widely in use throughout the world, there are certain aspects of them which can mislead operators. For instance, some purists argue that an advising bank has no right to issue a back-to-back credit against a foreign bank's credit without informing that bank. The implication here is that the applicant of the first credit is entitled to believe that he is buying the beneficiary's own goods. Whilst this may be the case where an importer is dealing for the first time with a foreign exporter and is unaware that he is a middleman, there is no excuse for him not obtaining up-to-date reports beforehand. A more important outcome from the use of these credits is the false level of creditworthiness which they bestow on the middleman. The beneficiary of a back-to-back credit or transferred credit may be under the misapprehension that the buyer, the middleman, has access to more extensive banking facilities than is actually the case; he is shown as the applicant and appears to be the opening bank's customer. Experienced exporters should be able to detect certain features which identify a credit as having been transferred or re-issued. The main danger lies in the opportunity for the middleman to exploit his apparent high level of creditworthiness and induce his suppliers to grant him credit on their own account. The view has been expressed by knowledgeable observers that the value of an irrevocable credit to a beneficiary is not so much the guarantee of payment, but satisfaction in the knowledge that he is selling to a buyer capable of obtaining adequate banking support.

The part payment credit

Buyers entering new markets or dealing for the first time with foreign suppliers are often understandably reluctant to place a large contract until they are confident of the seller's product. The part payment credit allows the buyer to withhold a percentage of the value of a shipment until its quality has been certified by independent cargo inspectors. It is opened payable as to, say, 80% against shipping documents and the balance after arrival of the carrying vessel and presentation of a quality certificate issued by the appointed inspectors at port of destination. This type of credit would have to be agreed upon in the buyer/seller contract and, although the seller may object that his cash flow will suffer from the delay in payment of the balance, as an alternative he can be asked to present a retention guarantee as a document required under the credit and draw 100% if his documents are in order. The retention guarantee has to be issued by an acceptable bank and be payable on demand by the buyer, supported by independent certification that the goods are not as detailed in the contract. Beneficiaries of these credits need to make sure that the issuing bank's irrevocable undertaking is for 100% of the value of the goods. If the credit is opened for less than 100%, then the clause relating to payment of the balance must make it clear that it will be made under the bank's responsibility. Finally, the credit must state which independent group will issue the inspection certificate; this should also have been agreed in the buyer/seller contract. If the credit is a usance credit, the beneficiary should be required to draw two drafts for each shipment, one for the amount payable against documents and one for the balance.

Chapter 9

Financing

Financing international trade in consumer goods is generally classified as short-term, the average credit being 180 days with exceptions running to 18 months. To understand the opportunities for banks to engage profitably in this type of finance it is necessary to examine the chain of contracts supporting most transactions. An importer seeking finance to purchase goods from overseas must satisfy his bank that he can liquidate any borrowing from the proceeds of the resale of those goods. The resale immediately becomes the most important aspect of the deal, so far as the bank is concerned, and can enable the bank to strengthen its security and increase its earnings; later in this chapter examples demonstrate this.

On the other side of the main contract, the supplier may require some degree of finance before he can forward his goods for shipment. That finance is generally to cover packing and transport, although he often buys in his goods from manufacturers before modifying and preparing them for specific buyers who may require their own trademarks to be added. Exporters and importers are rarely able to finance contracts simply by the use of a single method of payment such as an irrevocable credit.

Figures 9.1 and 9.2 illustrate the contractual relationships established between a foreign government, a Paris trader and a US supplier. The foreign government issues an invitation to tender for the supply of tallow which is advertised and transmitted to suppliers around the world. To ensure that interested suppliers are submitting genuine bids which they intend to honour, they are required to support their bid with a bid bond which they

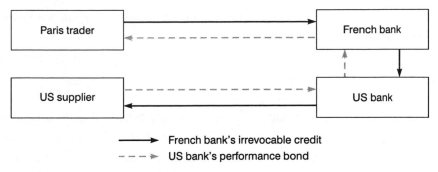

Figure 9.1 Financing Paris trader's purchase

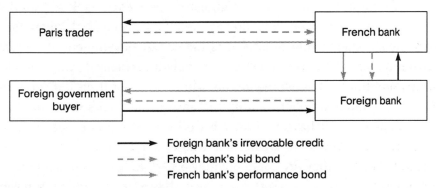

Figure 9.2 Financing Paris trader's sale

are told will automatically be converted into a performance bond if the bid is successful. Bid bonds are usually for 5% of the value of the contract and performance bonds are 10% and above. Immediately the Paris trader approaches his bank to obtain a bid bond, the bank realises the possible extent to which they may be required to provide finance if the trader's bid is successful. The minimum risk is the bid bond at 5% rising to 10% for a successful bid. Therefore, before issuing the bid bond, the bank requires certain assurances from their customer:

1 If your bid is successful, how will you be paid?
2 We are asked to guarantee that you will execute your contract with the foreign government, but where will you get the tallow from?
3 How will you pay for the tallow?

4 Are your terms of sale identical to the terms under which you are buying the tallow? If not, what are they?

5 Can you obtain a performance bond from your supplier to support our bond?

These are five basic questions; there are many technical ones which we will study when the whole operation is analysed and the various banking instruments are examined to ensure that they fully secure the banks. In the first instance, the invitation to tender will state by what method the successful bidder will be paid, almost certainly by irrevocable documentary credit issued by the foreign bank. The French bank will want to know whether the trader has already identified a source of tallow for a price which enables him to offer it to the foreign government at a profit. In many cases, a trader submits bids without actually having found a supply and the bank must rely on his skill to secure it if his bid succeeds. If he has found a supplier then he can answer the bank's third question, as the supplier will have indicated his price and requested payment by means of an irrevocable credit; but whose credit? If the trader's bank agrees to issue it, they are contemplating a back-to-back transaction using the foreign credit to support their own. However, government buyers frequently require credit for the purchase of commodities, so it is possible that the foreign credit will be a usance credit, available at up to 180 days from date of shipment. Unless the US supplier is prepared to offer similar terms to the Paris trader, his bank must decide whether it wishes to finance the gap. If the US supplier's terms are sight then the bank has to finance their customer for 180 days until maturity of the drafts under the foreign credit.

The reader will understand from the foregoing that few deals are as simple as they look and although the French bank, in this example, may decline to go any further than the issue of the performance bond, unless the trader is enabled to obtain and pay for his supply from the US, he may default on his contract with the foreign government and his performance bond will be called. The bank's skill lies in its ability to assess the obvious risks which we have highlighted and decide whether they outweigh the commissions and interest it will earn, in which case it is better to decline even to issue the bid bond.

For the purposes of this example, we will consider that the French bank elicits satisfactory answers from the trader to its questions and is prepared to finance his purchase and sale. A number of instruments are involved, all requiring careful scrutiny as to terms and availability.

1 A bid bond for $800 000 issued by the French Bank: if the bid is successful, this will become a performance bond for an amount of US$1 600 000.
2 Foreign government irrevocable credit issued by their bank for US $16 000 000 valid for 6 months and available by acceptance of 180 day drafts.
3 French bank irrevocable credit for US$15 650 000 in favour of the US supplier and available by payment at sight. This is the back-to-back credit and must be a reproduction of the foreign credit with alterations to amount, price, latest shipment date and validity, etc.
4 A bank performance bond from the US supplier for US$1 565 000. There are two ways in which this document can be obtained before the French bank becomes liable on its irrevocable credit. Firstly, it can demand receipt of the bond before it actually issues its credit. Secondly, and more practically, it can make it a condition of the credit that it only becomes operative once the bond has been presented to the nominated or advising bank. The bond must have a validity of at least 1 month beyond the expiry date of the French bank's credit.

The diagrams demonstrate the interdependence of the various instruments, but what they do not reveal are the political and technical risks which face the French bank. It is intending to lend up to $15 650 000 against the security of a foreign bank's irrevocable credit and, furthermore, once it has negotiated documents under that credit, it will have to wait 6 months before receiving payment for the 180 day drafts. As the advising bank for the foreign credit the French bank must be careful to study not only its terms but the question of confirmation. Ideally it should confirm the credit for two reasons. Firstly because, as the confirming bank, it will be entitled to object to any amendments which it cannot apply to the back-to-back credit. Secondly, by issuing the back-to-back credit it is assuming considerable risks for which, not unreasonably, the applicant should pay. When all these instruments are in force the first advising bank has to control their use in such a way that they fully support one another. If it manages to do that and if all the parties to this transaction meet their contractual liabilities on time, the only problem that could arise would be discrepancies in documents. However, default by the US supplier would present considerable difficulties for the French bank. The supplier would obviously ask for an extension to the back-to-back credit, but that credit must not be extended until the foreign bank's credit has been similarly extended.

Financing through bills for collection

The bill for collection, as a method of settlement, is not the most popular with banks due mainly to the volume of documents which they are required to handle and the small commissions they earn. Exporters who cannot persuade their buyers to establish documentary credits in their favour are obliged to use the collection, which is the next best thing. But they do not provide immediate payment and many exporters cannot afford to wait up to 1 month or more for settlement of collections. The reader will have understood from previous chapters that drawees are often able to delay payment of collections, sometimes up to the arrival of the carrying vessel. Banks are prepared to make advances to exporters secured by documents for collection on a revolving basis. The exporter provides the bank with a list of overseas buyers and details of the level of monthly shipments to them. Depending on the quality of the buyers and the political risk involved, the bank agrees to advance, say, 80% of monthly oustandings on each buyer that it approves. Where the collections are D/A and are avalised by a local bank acceptable to the exporter's bank, the amount advanced may be over 80%. The exporter prepares his documents for collection in the usual manner and hands them to his bank for collection. Now the bank has a financial interest in the documents and will check them thoroughly, ensuring that they are properly endorsed so as to give the bank a title to the goods and enable it to become an endorsee of the bill of exchange. This is a good point at which to demonstrate the value of Uniform Rules and the discipline they exert over the collecting bank in ensuring immediate notification of payment, acceptance, non-payment and non-acceptance. Once a D/P collection is paid, the exporter's bank is able to consider advancing against further bills and, if a D/A collection is accepted, it knows the date of maturity and can make provision for further advances at that time. If a D/P collection is not paid or a bill not accepted under a D/A collection, the exporter's bank is immediately on notice that the drawee may be in financial difficulties. It can stop advances on that particular buyer until it has obtained a report from the collecting bank. It takes all necessary precautions when financing collections to protect its security, and its original advice to the collecting bank includes instructions for the payment of freight (for FOB shipments), warehousing and insuring the goods in the event of non-payment or non-acceptance. If the importer has named a case of need, the bank liaises with that party to ensure that everything is done to persuade the drawee to take up the collection. In most cases, however, the bank simply recalls the advance made against that particular collection and leaves its customer to deal with any action necessary to protect the goods and find a new buyer. This situation highlights the risks to exporters whose goods lie unsold in a foreign country.

For this type of facility, the bank is greatly assisted if the exporter has export credit insurance which can be assigned to the bank. It will not necessarily grant facilities for advances to the full limits set by the insurers, who usually place an overall limit on buyers which may be spread across a number of exporters. Payment under these policies is generally limited to 90% of the amount claimed. When a policy is assigned to a bank, it must ensure that nothing prevents it from exercising its rights against the insurers. Consequently the bank has to keep a check on its customer to ensure that premiums are paid on time and that the customer does not fail to notify any shipments and is observing the policy limits. The bank must also ask for copies of all amendments to the policy which the insurers may make and the introduction of any excess. Monitoring advances presents administrative problems to the bank, but despite that this type of facility enables exporters to anticipate proceeds, acquire further goods for shipment and pay packing, warehousing and freight charges. If the exporter has export credit insurance, then that additional security for the bank is reflected in the rate of interest it charges. For undoubted exporters, collecting on approved buyers, some banks will advance against collections without seeing the documents, which it allows the customer to send direct to an approved collecting bank. It only remains then for the bank to periodically monitor its advances, which are liquidated by direct remittance to ensure that no items are unduly outstanding.

Negotiation of bills for collection

Whenever an exporter puts together a collection and draws a bill of exchange on his buyer, he is producing a source of finance. Banks are always prepared to negotiate collections, which means they actually buy the documents. There is no question of discounting because that practice requires the bill of exchange to have been accepted by the drawee or his bank; at the stage of a collection which we are considering, the bill of exchange has not been presented for payment or acceptance. Negotiation of bills for collection is different from advances against them in that the exporter or drawer is able to obtain 100% face value of the documents. The bank negotiates with full recourse to the drawer and credits him immediately. Eventually, upon payment of the collection abroad, the proceeds are remitted back to the exporter's bank which then debits him with interest from the date of negotiation to receipt of proceeds. Whenever banks take collections as security, they exercise care in examining the documents to ensure that they are correctly drawn and by endorsement pass a title to themselves. Additionally, the possibility of non-payment or non-acceptance and the resultant actions required to protect the goods mean that the bank will include protective clauses in its instructions to the collecting bank. However, when a collection is unpaid and protective action taken, the bank will ask its customer to repay the amount of the negotiation and leave him to deal with any legal action against the drawee, intervention by the case of need and possible resale of the goods.

Pre-shipment finance

Exporters preparing consignments for shipment or purchasing goods for resale to overseas buyers are frequently in need of finance before they can be paid for those goods. We have seen a number of instruments which assist exporters in this respect, namely the red and green clause credits and advance payment credits. Not all exporters, however, are fortunate enough to have the support of an irrevocable credit for their sales with or without advance payment terms.

Banks are able to assist their customers in this situation and provide finance in anticipation of eventual receipt of sale proceeds, but arranging security is not always easy. To illustrate the exporter's situation let us consider three scenarios.

In the first, the exporter has prepared and packed his goods for shipment, but has received no advice from his buyer concerning the method of payment, which he understands will be by D/P collection as agreed in the sales contract. He is confident of his buyer and wishes to arrange carriage and pay freight for a CFR shipment. The bank can advance the necessary funds to the exporter provided the goods are despatched to the bank's order with a forwarding agent who is instructed to arrange the issue of the bills of lading, also to the bank's order. The bank satisfies itself that the overseas buyer is creditworthy and asks the exporter to telex for confirmation regarding the settlement by D/P collection. From that point, the bank becomes a secured lender and handles the collection as remitting bank, except that the documents are suitably endorsed to protect its title to the goods.

In the second scenario, the exporter has a firm contract to sell to an overseas buyer and agrees to payment by 60 day D/A collection. In anticipation of eventual settlement by his buyer, the exporter wishes to purchase a variety of goods which will be packed into a container for shipment. However, his local suppliers are not prepared to extend him credit for more than a short period and certainly not for the 60 days' credit allowed to the foreign buyer. The key to the bank's decision whether or not to finance the exporter's local purchases lies in the quality of his buyer and the political risks involved. If the reports that the bank obtains on the buyer are satisfactory it can dispense with any need for the term bill of exchange to be avalised as that process does not reduce the political risk; it only eliminates the risk of non-payment. The bank therefore makes its decision based entirely on the political risk and, if it is acceptable, proceeds to arrange finance for the exporter. Security is the most important element of this transaction and the bank will be anxious to ensure that at all times it maintains control over the goods. In this example, the bank insists that any goods purchased by the exporter are stored in an approved warehouse against warehouse warrants in the bank's name. That warehouse is appointed to pack the container, have it marked to the overseas buyer and delivered it to the port of shipment by a forwarding agent. The bills of lading for eventual shipment are issued to the order of the bank and will form part of the D/A collection. By this method, the bank enables its customer to pay for goods and services at sight and finances the gap between those payments and the ultimate receipt of proceeds under the D/A collection. It is really a chain of different forms of security: from warehouse warrant to bill of lading and, eventually, a bill of exchange accepted by an approved buyer.

Finally, an exporter who is the beneficiary of an irrevocable credit which is not transferable and does not allow pre-shipment advances, is buying the relative goods from a supplier in his own country; that supplier wishes to be paid at sight. UCP600 Article 39 allows the beneficiary to assign any proceeds to which he may become entitled under a credit. It is important to stress that a documentary credit cannot itself be assigned and, although assignment of its proceeds is permitted, the fact that a credit is a conditional guarantee means that an assignee must rely on the beneficiary complying fully with its terms. In the case which we are considering, the assignment can be executed two ways. The proceeds may be assigned to the exporter's suppliers, but they will not be paid until documents are presented under the credit. A more satisfactory solution is for the assignment to be in favour of the bank, who can then advance funds to pay local suppliers. Care must be taken to ensure that local laws are complied with in the execution of the assignment. The reader will understand the importance, when agreeing the terms of their contract, for exporters to demand a method of payment which facilitates pre-shipment finance to avoid having to make last-minute arrangements with their own banks.

Post-shipment finance

The fact that an importer has been financed to pay his overseas supplier does not necessarily mean that he can immediately repay the bank providing that finance. When goods are imported they undergo a number of processes before reaching the final buyer. On arrival, freight may have to be paid and the goods transported and warehoused pending re-packing and distribution. During this period, the importer is often forced to depend on his bank for finance for whatever charges he incurs, and possibly for any credit he has extended to his buyers. The reader should appreciate that when a bank issues an irrevocable documentary credit on behalf of its customer, it is virtually agreeing to make a loan when documents are presented by the negotiating bank, unless the applicant is able to take them up immediately for cash. By honouring a claim under its credit, the bank creates a loan against documents of title, which, after discharge of the carrying vessel, becomes an advance against goods. Only on disposal of the relative goods and payment by the final buyers can the advance be repaid but then only provided that they are not buying on credit. There is a logical sequence to the stages of finance required for imported goods, with the bank endeavouring to maintain its security right through until final settlement. The bank relies on the operators we have highlighted earlier: forwarding agents, warehousemen and inland carriers. Where goods are on-sold by the importer on credit terms, the bank will seek to secure itself by having bills of exchange drawn in its favour and accepted by the buyers, who it must approve. The bank will also insist that any form of credit insurance the importer has on his domestic buyers is assigned to it, or at least that its interest is noted by the insurers.

Whatever the means are by which an importer expects to be paid by his buyers, and despite any credit he is extending to them, banks can generally finance the gap between import and final receipt of proceeds. The reader will recall the questions which a bank may ask when receiving a request to open an import credit, particularly regarding the final disposition of the goods and method of payment for them. Each method offers the bank a different level of security, with the irrevocable credit, established in the importer's favour by his buyers, being the most acceptable. When this happens, the bank should try to have the credit advised through itself, thus gaining full control over the goods until the credit is honoured. This is a form of back-to-back credit except that the bank does not necessarily set out to match the two credits. In addition to being able to recoup its advances by using the final buyer's credit, the bank may earn commissions for advising, possibly confirming and for negotiating it.

In many cases, credits are issued covering goods consigned direct to countries outside the applicant's country of residence; this is trading or merchanting and it can only be financed if the issuing bank is satisfied with the method of payment by the foreign buyer. Although the procedures are similar to those applied to domestic sales, the possibility of political risk arises. Consequently an issuing bank relying on a foreign credit or a collection has to assess that risk before entering into the transaction. It may, for example, insist that the foreign credit be confirmed or that a collection be avalised and any insurance on the buyer assigned to the bank.

While banks are always prepared to assist their customers as much as possible with finance for imports, difficulties arise when the goods have to be processed by a third party before being despatched to the final buyer. A good example is the import of skins and leather which require treating, colouring and cutting before becoming acceptable products. When such items enter the processor's factory, the bank's title virtually disappears and it must rely on the reputation of the processor, from whom it may be prepared to get an undertaking that immediately processing is completed, the goods will only be released on the bank's instructions.

Assignment/purchase of trade receivables

This type of facility, which is operated by both banks and factoring companies, does not rely on the use of bills of exchange. It is a straightforward financing of an exporter's book debts.

The main features are that the bank or factoring company is providing credit to exporters and buyers against the security of the exporter's claim on the overseas buyers in open account trading. It is a revolving facility linked to the value of total debts outstanding at any one time and credit is given for an agreed percentage of those debts. The creditworthiness of buyer and seller is of paramount importance.

There are, however, important differences between the facilities operated by banks and those operated by factors. First and foremost, banks provide credit to the seller (exporter) and factors provide credit to the buyer (importer)

Thus when using an accounts receivable facility with a bank, the exporter is still liable for the risk of non-payment by the buyer, the transfer risk, the political risk and the exchange risk, i.e. the bank has full recourse to the exporter.

Factors, however, actually **buy** the exporter's book debts and assume responsibility for the commercial and political risks, leaving the exporter with a liability for the transfer risk and the exchange risk. In some cases, the factor will also assume liability for the transfer and exchange risks.

One area where exporters may prefer to use a bank facility rather than factoring, concerns their relationship with their overseas buyers. The bank deals solely with the exporter and rarely takes an assignment on the book debts, whereas factors finance the buyers, deal with them direct and take an assignment of debts. Many exporters may not wish their buyers to know what their financial arrangements are. Giving an assignment over book debts can be interpreted as a sign of financial weakness, which some buyers might seek to exploit.

Chapter 10

Forfaiting

Forfaiting or **without-recourse financing** is a method of trade finance whereby the forfaiting bank purchases, on a without-recourse basis, unconditional debt obligations arising from the provision of goods and/or services which are due to mature at a future date. The term originates from *à forfait* finance which simply means that the exporter forfeits all rights to future receivables in exchange for immediate payment.

In a forfait transaction, therefore, the exporter agrees to surrender the rights to claim for payment of goods or services delivered to an importer under a contract of sale, in return for a cash payment from a forfaiting bank. In exchange for the payment, the forfaiting bank takes over the exporter's debt instruments and thereafter assumes the full risk of payment by the importer. The exporter is, in the circumstances, absolved of financial involvement in the transaction and is liable only on the quality and reliability of the project.

Underlying a forfaiting transaction is a contract for the supply of goods and/or services whereby the supplier/exporter grants to the buyer/importer credit terms of payment. In the past, forfaiting only applied to the financing of capital equipment, but nowadays financing of commodities, especially oil, by this method is common. Forfaiting is also no longer perceived as a medium-term financing tool and is suitable for periods as short as 120 days. Depending on country risk and amounts involved, shorter or longer terms under different repayment programmes can be considered. The repayment instalments are, as a rule, composed of principal and interest payments over the agreed period of financing. Transaction amounts considered usually start from as low as US$250 000 up to a maximum of tens of millions of US

Dollars. Apart from US Dollars, other acceptable currencies are UK Sterling, the Euro and Swiss Franc. An important basic rule on without-recourse financing or non-recourse financing is that the debt purchased by the forfaiting bank represents an unconditional payment obligation. It must be separate and independent from the underlying exporter transaction, to avoid any possible future objections on commercial grounds. The debt should in addition be freely transferable. As a rule, the forfaiting bank requires the debt purchased to be secured by a bank guarantee on an unconditional, on-demand and freely transferable basis. The guarantor bank is usually a first-class bank in the buyer's/importer's country. This requirement is waived only in circumstances where the buyer is itself a prime buyer, such as a government agency or a major multinational company.

Documentation for forfaiting transactions is usually in the form of promissory notes, bills of exchange, book receivables or deferred payments under a letter of credit. Promissory notes are issued by the buyer/importer to the order of the supplier/exporter and endorsed by the latter to the order of the forfaiting bank. Bills of exchange are drawn by the seller/exporter to his order on the buyer/importer and accepted by the buyer/importer. They are then endorsed to the order of the forfaiting bank. The notes and bills are usually guaranteed by a first-class bank on the paper itself with their endorsement or with the wording 'per aval for account of . . .' (name of buyer/importer).

When a forfaiting bank agrees to buy a transaction from a supplier/exporter, it does so for cash at an agreed discount rate, based on LIBOR for the relevant currency and term, plus a spread or margin. This spread or margin is determined by the political risk involved. In addition, the acceptability of the risk on the non-recourse financing market has to be taken into consideration. It is important to note that the level of discount rate for a particular risk can be strongly influenced by the prevailing market situation and sentiments, not related to the facts mentioned above. The discount rate can be applied on either a **straight discount** or **discount to yield** basis. A simple example best illustrates the difference between the two discounting methods.

A straight discount of 10% pa applied to a bill of US$1 000 000 is US$100 000. The net sum after discount is US$900 000. If the bill matures after 1 year this represents an effective yield or discount to yield rate of 11.11% pa (i.e. 100/900), compounded annually.

The discount margin is the one major cost component of a forfaiting transaction. The only other cost element involved is the commitment fee. It should be pointed out that in certain cases, and depending on the nature and country of the transaction, several days of grace may be included in computing the interest to be deducted, i.e. the discount is deducted for some additional days beyond maturity. Days of grace are often added as extra discount because experience will have shown the forfaiting bank that the particular guarantor bank usually pays a number of days after due date. Some of the advantages of forfaiting to the exporter can be summarized as follows:

■ conversion of a credit transaction into a cash transaction
■ elimination of all political and credit risks
■ simple documentation
■ improve liquidity
■ elimination of exchange risks.

For the importer, forfaiting gives him the flexibility to pay for his goods on deferred terms of credit and at a fixed interest cost.

Forfaiting is a financial technique designed to meet the challenge of difficult markets, and although several of the areas to which it was best applied originally now trade without the need to seek medium- to long-term finance, it still has an important role to play in international trade. Export credit agencies (ECAs) have been forced to put their business on a more commercial footing which, coupled with a shift away from official support for exporters, has led to a heightened perception of the political and economic risks facing them. Cover can therefore be difficult to acquire in what are otherwise valuable markets. Forfaiting can provide a way for exporters to finance sales to valued corporate clients even in the most difficult circumstances. While a national ECA may have reached the ceiling of its country cover, a forfaiter may have just the required amount of finance available. Even when ECA cover is available, but not for down payment and other associated costs, forfaiting can provide the finance. Goods financed can include commodities, capital equipment, spare parts and services which may originate from any country because, unlike ECAs, forfaiters face no restrictions concerning the origin of goods. Where an export has been agreed for a forfait finance, if it should be frustrated the finance can still be available if the goods are sold internally. Please refer to Figure 10.1.

Project financing for projects requiring up to 8 years' finance can be arranged through forfaiting. In addition, **pre-export finance** allows exporters to finance local purchases prior to export and bridges the gap between sourcing and receipt of proceeds from overseas buyers. It is, in fact, the equivalent of the red and green clause documentary credits. Of considerable benefit to exporters is the fact that a forfaiter, once a contract has been finalized with a foreign buyer, provides the exporter with a fixed rate commitment from which point all future political and interest rate risks are removed, provided the exporter adheres to the conditions on documentation.

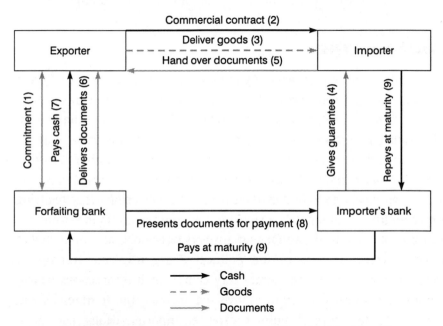

1   The exporter is provided with a firm written commitment that its claim will be purchased by the forfaiting bank.
2   Commercial contract is signed.
3   Goods are delivered.
4   Guarantee is released (or L/C is confirmed as being operative).
5 & 6   Documents are released to the exporter by the importer and then endorsed or assigned to the forfaiting bank.
7   The forfaiting bank discounts the face value of documents and pays the net proceeds to the exporter.
8   At maturity, documents are presented for collection to the guaranteeing or L/C issuing bank.
9   Repayment of face value takes place.

Figure 10.1   Typical forfaiting transaction procedure

Forfaiting paper: an active market exists in bills of exchange and promissory notes which have been issued to support forfaiting deals and have become the property of the forfaiter. In such form they represent relatively liquid assets and can be an attractive investment offering a higher yield than other medium-term instruments. The yield must be seen in relation to the political risk and the fact that the resale of forfaited claims is always made without recourse. Due to the fact that these instruments are usually only available in relatively large tranches, it is the large investors who are most active in the market. Forfaiting is carried out at fixed rates and consequently upward movements in interest rates create a demand for the paper. In contrast, when interest rates are low forfaiting declines, as the opportunity to substitute medium-term risks for cash is less attractive.

Countertrade

Countertrade covers a wide range of techniques for handling reciprocal trade which will be analysed and explained in this chapter. Principally, most countertrade deals enable export sales to be made to particular markets on condition that undertakings are given to purchase goods from those markets. Simple barter, that is the exchange of goods for goods of another nature, is now relatively rare; methods have been devised to assist countries with little or no foreign exchange to find markets for their goods using deals involving several countries. Countertrade, in one form or another, is said to account for almost 20% of world trade, although many very large deals are conducted in complete secrecy because of the political issues involved. It employs specialist operators who can handle very complicated transactions which, because of the number of countries involved, increase the commercial and political risks far beyond normal exporter/importer deals. For some countries, countertrade is the only way in which they can enter foreign markets, earn foreign exchange and purchase essential equipment, plant and technology to improve their economies. However, it is not always the poorer countries for whom countertrade creates benefits. Exporters in wealthy western countries frequently find that competition, price cutting and political embargoes make it difficult for them to dispose of their products. By using countertrade, they can effectively sell to countries which are unable to pay directly in foreign exchange. An additional benefit to exporters arises from the reduction in the pressures of competition and market forces which countertrade can produce. Instead of being forced into uneconomic price reductions in order to remain in some markets, manufacturers and traders can trade with poor countries using goods-based transactions which will give a return at normal price levels. Concessions have to be made by exporters and importers and reciprocity levels agreed between them.

The principal types of countertrade are:

- offset: direct and indirect
- compensation
- buy back
- counterpurchase
- bilateral agreements using clearing accounts
- switch trading
- tolling
- co-operation agreements
- build – operate – transfer

Offset

This is one of the most popular forms of countertrade, generally involving government intervention in co-production. Consequently there is a heavy emphasis on the supply and procurement of military equipment of all types. Offsets can be direct or indirect. Direct offset involves the transfer to the importing country of, for example, technology relating to the production of aircraft, transport and telecommunication systems. The introduction of advanced know-how enables the importer to update its systems while still using local labour and resources. Under an indirect offset, the selling country agrees to purchase materials and products from the importing country in order to improve its trade balances. Although those materials may not be related to the technology it has provided, the exporting country can benefit from their use in re-exports.

Improved quality goods, now produced by the importing country as a result of introducing higher-level technology, command a wider international market with increased earnings in foreign exchange. Offset agreements extend to the introduction of advanced control systems, management training, production line technology and civil engineering methods. Exporters have to exercise caution when entering into supply contracts which initially do not appear to require them to undertake offset obligations. In some instances suppliers have been successful in their bid only to find that the importing country then discloses an offset requirement which obliges the suppliers to purchase local products. Cautious exporters usually make discreet enquiries about the type and quality of products available in the importing country and ascertain whether there are markets for them in other countries. An exporter, desperate to get a foothold in a foreign country but unable to dispose of any products under an offset obligation, may pass that obligation to a third party, known as an offset house. Obviously, it is preferable for offset arrangements to be declared at the beginning of negotiation between supplier and importer otherwise their subsequent inclusion may render the deal unprofitable.

Some governments, and in particular the UK government, place restrictions on the countries with whom they will agree the imposition of offsets in relation to contracts carried out in the civil sector. For obvious reasons, they have to protect their own industries against excessive imports of foreign products. However, if the importer is a developing country, then an offset proposal may be accepted.

Compensation

Compensation agreements, in a variety of forms, are arrangements whereby the importing country settles its contract with the supplier part in foreign exchange and the balance in goods, produce and services. Where possible, the exporter will try to take back goods which are a direct product of the machinery or technology that he has supplied. In that way he at least has a product which he is accustomed to selling to established buyers. It is not always necessary in compensation agreements for the exporting country to provide its goods first; for seasonal and marketing reasons, it may be preferable to dispose of goods from the importing country while the exporting country is preparing its compensating goods. As with offsets, where the exporting country is anxious to secure a contract, it may be able to find a third country prepared to take goods from the importing country which could otherwise be difficult to sell. This situation demonstrates the problems which face exporters who, although obliged to accept goods in part settlement of their contracts, find that having no control over their manufacture often results in poor quality products unacceptable in their traditional markets. Where possible, exporters of capital equipment and machinery will provide training of operatives and supervision of production at the initial stages. This is particularly important where the end product can be linked to the exporter, possibly by trade name and, any reduction in quality may damage his market reputation. See Figures 10.2 and 10.3.

Compensation with assignment allows the principal supplier to deliver his goods on credit and for the importer's debt to be assigned to a trader. When the principal supplier has identified acceptable compensation goods, he has the option to either take physical delivery or sell them to the trader. The trader takes a premium for his participation and pays the principal supplier in foreign exchange. Cancellation of the assignment is automatic upon delivery of the compensation goods. As an alternative to taking an assignment, the principal supplier can ask for a suitable bank performance bond from the importer to cover the delivery delay. See Figure 10.4.

Buy back

These agreements provide for an exporter to supply plant, equipment and technology and, once installation has been completed, to buy back products from its operation. The exporter is recompensed entirely through product, although provision may be made for part cash settlement. The dangers to an exporter in having to take exclusively product from the equipment he has supplied, arise when production levels fall or if production is halted due to industrial action. Any sales made in anticipation

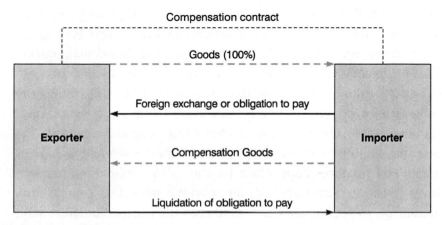

Figure 10.2 Full compensation

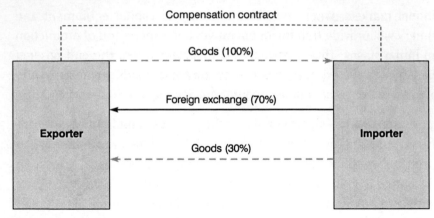

Figure 10.3 Partial compensation

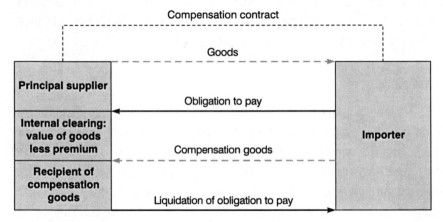

Figure 10.4 Compensation with assignment

of the output will be affected. Buy back deals can run for up to 20 years, during which time renovation, replacement, upgrading and redesigning must be carried out regularly by the supplier in order to maintain quality levels. The benefits of these agreements are equally divided between importing and exporting countries. The importer can rely on the supplier to equip factories which guarantee a certain level of local employment. Local investment is then concentrated on marketing, packing and exporting. The exporter has an overseas investment, using possibly cheaper labour and raw materials that produce goods which he can sell in established markets. However, there is always the danger that the importing country may eventually be competing in world markets with cheaper products than those offered by the suppliers of its plant and machinery.

Counterpurchase

As its title suggests, this is an agreement between an exporter, known as the principal supplier, and an importer to purchase goods from each other. Principally, the exporter supplies, for example, essential machinery, parts, materials and chemicals required to support the importer's industries. Unlike offset and buy back, the goods on both sides of the transaction are settled in foreign exchange, although in cases where the exporter has no market for the other parties' goods he may be allowed to nominate a third-party buyer. The method is particularly attractive to countries with limited foreign exchange, allowing them to update and maintain plant and machinery essential to their export programmes. So far as the principal supplier is concerned, counterpurchase gives him much greater freedom of choice. By comparison, being tied in a long-term buy back can result in the exporter having to find alternative outlets for the limited range of goods available to him as demand in his domestic market declines. In essence, the counterpurchase agreement is simply a contract for the sale and purchase of specific goods over an agreed period. The counterpurchase obligation is not a part of the original contract but is a separate agreement allowing the supplier considerable latitude in selection of counterpurchase goods. An element of risk confronts the principal supplier who may find that the importer defaults on the delivery of goods which he, the principal supplier, has contracted to sell on or which he relies on as materials for his own manufacturing units. This is a possible outcome of a substantial rise in world prices, when the importer is tempted to redirect counterpurchase goods to a more profitable market. Falling quality, delays in delivery and market competition are extremely difficult for the principal supplier to exercise any control over. In many cases his situation is not helped by the fact that his counter-party is several thousand miles away. The operation of a counterpurchase agreement is quite straight-forward, beginning with a contract of sale and purchase between the two parties, whose contractual obligations are usually executed by the use of irrevocable documentary credits. Performance guarantees may be demanded on both sides to protect against non-delivery and, where either party elects to transfer its counterpurchase commitment to a trading house, the commission payable is often the subject of an on-demand guarantee. Trading houses are specialists in counterpurchase and will undertake to be responsible for either side of the agreement. They have access to extensive markets and, for a commission, will source goods and find buyers for those goods unacceptable to either party for the counterpurchase agreement.

Contracts

There are two distinctly separate contracts in a counterpurchase deal. The first is the principal sale contract between the supplier and the importer which covers the sale and purchase of agreed goods or services. Settlement of each parties' obligations under that contract is in no way dependent upon any counterpurchase arrangement. The second contract relates to the counterpurchase and stipulates the extent to which the principal supplier is obliged to buy goods from the importer; it does not necessarily have to be for an amount equal to the first contract. Where the principal supplier is unable or unwilling to import the counterpurchase goods, a third contract between him and a trading house is established under which, for a commission, the trading house finds an alternative buyer. This is a specialist area in which the principal supplier may lack the experience and legal knowledge necessary to make counterpurchase arrangements direct with a third party buyer; he is better off leaving such dealings to a specialist and paying their commission. Multinationals, however, are in a strong position when confronted with the need to find counterpurchase parties, often being able to select buyers in their own groups.

Bilateral agreements

Bilateral agreements are designed to develop and consolidate countertrade between two countries and are generally agreed at government level. They vary from firm commitments, which specify the extent of participation by each party and may stipulate the type of goods to be traded, to loose political agreements intended to build trade relationships. They are generally established with a view to reducing the outflow of foreign exchange by using clearing currencies. This is the first mention made of clearing currencies and the reader should understand that clearing or switch currencies are merely book entries in a special account held in a third country. An exporter selling to an importer in a switch deal earns units in a clearing currency which are credited to his account. The only way he can use that balance is either to purchase goods from a country which also has a clearing currency account or to sell it to a switch trader for conversion into foreign exchange. With bilateral agreements both parties agree to a level of countertrade which, over a given period of time, should balance out. They are usually for large undertakings whereby, for example, an industrial nation builds power stations for a country prepared to supply raw materials in exchange: oil, coal and natural gas are typical of the products involved. Upon completion of an agreement, either by time expiry or because the levels of countertrade have been reached, each party is free to settle any credit or debit balance it has accumulated in a clearing account. The accounts act as a monitor during the countertrade period and may be frozen if one party exceeds the agreed trade imbalance and incurs a debit balance. It then has to step up its exports to liquidate the balance at which point its trading partner can resume exporting.

Switch trading

Switch trading can be the natural outcome of a number of countertrade practices where the exporter cannot be paid in foreign exchange: the buyer is either short of foreign exchange or has built up a balance in a clearing currency which he would rather use to settle imports than sell to a switch trader. By agreement, the exporter sells goods to the importer and allows him to pay in a clearing currency. Because clearing currencies are not convertible, the exporter puts a premium on the price of his goods to counter the commission he pays to eventually sell the clearing currency balance he has accumulated. For the exporter there is always the risk that the switch trader finds it difficult to locate buyers who are prepared to buy goods from a country using clearing currencies. See Figure 10.5.

Tolling

The ability to meet production and delivery targets on time presents one of the biggest challenges to some of the manufacturing units in Eastern Europe and the Far East. The reader will remember the importance placed on the risk of non-delivery in cross-border trading, resulting in the calling of performance bonds and other obligations. It is easy to see that a regular and reliable supply of raw materials is essential if these plants are to meet their commitments, and shortage of foreign exchange can endanger those supplies. Tolling is a technique whereby an exporter or financial institution agrees to supply raw materials to a plant in a foreign country and to buy the

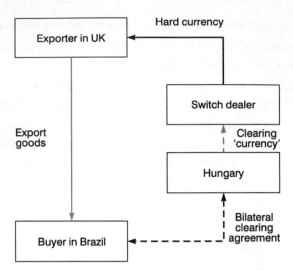

Figure 10.5 Switch in simple form

end product: aluminium, steel and copper are typical materials involved in tolling. The process benefits both parties; the producer is able to maintain production and eventual sales without using foreign exchange to buy his raw materials. By assuming a degree of control over the plant, the supplier assures himself of a supply of the finished products, possibly at favourable prices. He retains ownership of the raw materials during processing, although there are a number of problems which may confront him before the end product is available to him. Most tolling agreements are comparatively long-term so political and economic changes are possible, causing interruption of production, switching of sales to strategic markets to meet political pressures and even moving towards importing a cheaper product under bilateral agreements. The supplier of materials in a tolling arrangement must exercise close supervision of the plant or factory, taking performance guarantees where possible to protect his projected sales of end-products. Where the plant produces steel, copper, aluminium and the like, the product can be sold forward to protect against world price movements and futures markets exist to allow the supplier to hedge his sales. Although the supplier may take a financial interest in the plant and maintain ownership of his materials during production, a strong element of goodwill must exist if he is really to feel secure. Any form of charge over materials which change physically and lose their identity in processing is always difficult to enforce.

Co-operation agreements

Co-operation agreements go far beyond mere trading and can include military, political, industrial and commercial arrangements between two countries. The countertrade aspect is simply a by-product of such agreements and serves as a method of settling the obligations of both parties. For example, a general agreement to exchange technical know-how can include permission from a manufacturer of farm tractors to allow them to be produced in a foreign country, but strictly to his own specification. The overall co-operation agreement may be almost wholly of an agricultural nature but with the tractors providing an essential uplift in the country's farming techniques. Compensation for the tractor manufacturer may take several forms as payment in foreign exchange is unlikely. Surplus production over and above the importing country's own requirements is available for other markets, possibly at prices below those of the original tractors due to lower labour costs. A percentage of export proceeds, as agreed between the parties, provides payment for the obligation due to the original manufacturer. However, it is essential that limits are agreed on levels of exports by the foreign producer and the countries to which they may be sold, otherwise the original manufacturer may find himself in competition with an identical produce that has the benefit of certain cheaper cost elements.

Build – operate – transfer

This is a form of project finance designed to assist countries wishing to introduce essential services for their population but who lack the foreign exchange to pay for power stations, hydroelectricity schemes and similar undertakings; neither do they have the necessary technical skills. By engaging a foreign contractor to carry out the work and to agree to operate the unit once it has been completed, the buyer creates income from the resultant product. That income is projected over the required number of years to fully repay the contractor. The importer is eventually left with a unit which will considerably improve its economy and raise the standard of living. By agreement, such contracts often provide for a continued level of supervision after the payment period has expired and the debt has been liquidated. These deals are extremely difficult to put together, particularly where several contractors are involved, often from different countries. The reader will recognize the problems which can arise from the required performance bond being subject to a variety of national laws and the variations in payment terms between the parties. Political risk is high when a project is spread over a number of years and contractors will not assume it without some form of export credit insurance.

Legal issues

Legal issues relating to countertrade deals are often extremely complicated and responsible for the length of time required for the parties to reach agreement. When contracts are first drawn up, it is important that they contain all the details of the countertrade agreement because each contract will determine the commitment of each party. To that end, the contracts should set out the individual methods of payment, the exact details of the goods or services to be supplied on either side, and provisions to cover non-delivery, late delivery and failure to perform due to *force majeure*. It is also essential that the parties to the countertrade agreement recognize the need for any litigation which may arise to be dealt with by international commercial arbitration rather than national courts. The reason is simple: legal requirements may be completely different in each of the parties' countries and recourse to law would be unduly protracted and expensive. Commercial arbitration bodies exist to consider disputes in all trade-related transactions, and that includes countertrade. Arbitrators apply the same rules and legal principles as national courts but they enjoy two distinct advantages over them. Firstly, the arbitration panel comprises trade experts from commodity houses, financial institutions, shipping companies and other agencies servicing international trade. Secondly, they do not have a host of other commercial cases to consider as is generally the case in the law courts; hence the time taken for the parties to get a hearing is drastically reduced. Another important aspect of arbitration is that, without the use of expensive legal representation, it is considerably less expensive than taking a case to court.

Supporting countertrade deals is effected by using most of the instruments and techniques discussed in previous chapters. At some stage of a deal it is not difficult to imagine the parties having recourse to bid and performance bonds, standby credits and a variety of forms of documentary credits.

Barter

This is how trade, domestic and cross-border, began: the exchange of goods and services between two trading parties. Nowadays direct barter is rarely practised, but the introduction of a third party in a deal can enable trade between two countries to be settled without the use of money. The two parties to the barter may be unable to fully accept the goods each has to offer; sometimes because the quantity cannot be absorbed in the domestic market, or because the quality makes them unacceptable. By introducing a third-country buyer, prepared to take unwanted goods at a discount, the barter parties can complete their deal. The risk in involving a third party, who may eventually find alternative supplies at lower prices and of a higher quality, effectively limits the length of a barter contract. All three parties should agree renewals on an annual basis.

Case study

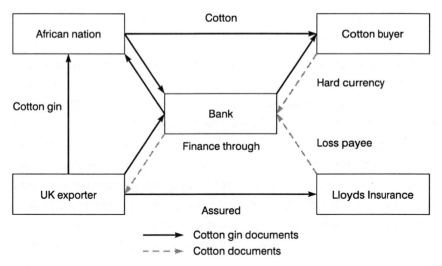

Figure 10.6 Case history of a recent countertrade deal (buy back)

This example concerns an African country which is a major producer of cotton. The country's cotton production was growing, but the state industry was being hampered as it needed to buy new cotton gins to expand its processing. A UK firm wanted to supply the gins, but the African client could not raise credit or satisfy the supplier's export credit agency. The solution was to structure a countertrade deal as follows.

The basic idea was to use part of the production of 2 year's cotton crop to pay for a cotton gin costing £5 million – this amount of cotton could be supplied with disrupting the country's normal cotton trading pattern.

The countertrader had now identified a viable product, but this would still have to be turned into cash. To do this, a buyer for the cotton was found, and a contract drawn up to sell the cotton 2 years forward. Locating a buyer who regularly bought cotton from that country helped significantly in achieving this. On this basis the cotton purchaser could now open letter of credit in support of its contract, and payment for the gin could then be effected by the bank discounting bills of exchange drawn under the credits.

However there were still two fundamental risks to take into account: the availability of the cotton, and the risks associated with its delivery. The African delivery risk was relatively easy – this could be covered through private insurance markets, such as Lloyds. The availability of the raw cotton was more of a problem – cover for crop failure is not as simple or as effective as other forms of insurance.

If the deal was to proceed, the UK gin supplier needed to be satisfied that this risk was acceptably small. To do this, it was important to ensure that the ratios were right; for example, if £5 million represented 90% of the client's cotton exports, then there would be no margin for error – one failed crop (due to a single climatic disaster or human error) would mean no cotton for export and therefore no repayment for the gin. However, in this case, the countertrader was able to verify that the percentage was very much smaller, and that the raw cotton would come from dispersed areas – so that a single disaster would only affect part of the crop.

Source: UK Department of Trade and Industry

Let us examine the complete operational cycle of the countertrade deal shown in Figure 10.6 and identify the traditional instruments of trade finance on which it relies and which have been discussed in previous chapters.

1 The UK exporter arranges insurance against possible non-delivery of cotton by the African state industry and assigns the insurance cover to the countertrader.

2 When that insurance is in place, the cotton buyer is asked to establish an irrevocable documentary credit or credits in favour of the countertrader, valid for 2 years.

3 On the strength of that credit, the countertrader can now authorize the UK exporter to despatch the cotton gin to the African state industry.

4 In the first year, the African state industry ships cotton to the cotton buyer and sends the documents to the countertrader.

5 The countertrader presents the documents against the documentary credit, which we must assume is a usance one as the diagram states that the bills are discounted.

6 The UK exporter is paid from the proceeds of the discounted bills.

7 In the second year, stages (4), (5) and (6) are repeated until the UK exporter has been paid £5 million.

This is a complex deal and raises several points which the reader may have already observed.

■ The UK exporter will charge interest on the cost of the cotton gin from the time of despatch. Interest will be payable on £5 million until the first payment under the cotton buyer's credit and thereafter reducing balances as further shipments of cotton are made.

■ If the cotton buyer is only a short sea journey from the African supplier, the documents of title may have to go direct to the buyer or to the issuing bank instead of via the countertrader. In that situation, the obvious solution would be to use a standby credit instead of a documentary credit due to the absence of bills of lading.

■ The cotton buyer is paying in Sterling for his cotton and faces an exchange risk, spread possibly over 2 years. Currency options would, at least, fix his liabilities.

This whole deal would be expensive and time-consuming to set up; it demonstrates the high level of skill required from the countertrader.

Chapter 11

Electronic commerce for international trade settlement

Banking, over the past 20 years, has moved rapidly towards the use of electronic systems, particularly in the movement of funds where SWIFT has been the greatest development, providing instantaneous transfers across the world. It was only a matter of time before operators in international trade began to examine possibilities of speeding up the transfer of documents. Faster vessels have reduced voyage times with the result that, very often, carrying steamers arrive at their destinations before the documents required to clear the cargo. Many indemnities have been required to enable consignees to obtain their goods without incurring charges for delays in unloading at ports of destination but, apart from the use of couriers (often expensive) the movement of shipping documents is no quicker than it was 50 years ago.

A group of interested parties, comprised of shipping companies, banks, forwarding agents, insurers and SWIFT have been engaged in a project intended to find an alternative method for the production and transmission of documents. Such a system had to meet a number of criteria before it could be introduced commercially and 'sold' to international trade operators. The system must be fast, secure, confidential and flexible.

Bolero

Bolero is the product of the project mentioned above and has been developed for introduction into international trade. Those responsible have formed a governing body entitled **Bolero Association Ltd** and all operators, in whatever field of international trade they are engaged, will be able to use the system provided they become subscribers. As users of the system they would be required to agree to the operating rules by signing the Rulebook, which sets the relationship between Association members.

Bolero provides:

1 an electronic commerce service
2 a core messaging platform
3 access through the use of internet
4 title registry
5 high level security using cryptographic technology
6 digital signing of messages limiting access only to authorized users
7 a liability policy to protect carriers and exporters against, inter alia, loss of interest, charter costs, demurrage and customs costs.

Primarily, Bolero is intended to eliminate 'paper documents' and replace them by electronically produced documents capable of being sent by electronic means.

The benefits of this aspect alone are very considerable if we consider the weaknesses of the paper method.

1 Documents are often delayed by using airmail and can be lost, if not permanently, certainly for long enough to cause the banks and consignees great inconvenience and expense.
2 Manually produced documents offer opportunities for fraud through forgery, alteration and unauthorized amendment.
3 Documents which were found to be out of order, could not, in many cases be corrected manually and re-presented to banks within the validity of their respective irrevocable credits (time is money!).
4 Importers and exporters were unable to cover foreign exchange commitments until the documents were found by both negotiating and issuing banks to be in order.
5 Communication between the various parties to a transaction was limited to the exchange of mail and fax messages where opinions were sought as to the authenticity or correctness of a given document or documents.

In addition to speed of settlement, Bolero will reduce opportunity for fraud and improve beneficiaries' chances of correcting discrepancies in documents in order for them to be negotiated within an imminently expiring credit. It will enable issuing banks to have documents corrected that were issued thousands of miles away.

How will it work?

1 Subscribers to the scheme will be able to raise their documents electronically, whether for collection or for presentation against a documentary credit, and to submit them electronically (EDI).
2 All documents transmitted will be protected by the use of a 'private key' agreed between parties for authentication purposes.
3 Recipients of transmissions will confirm that the content appears to be complete and correct (an essential reservation for banks receiving documents in which they have a financial interest and contractual liabilities towards beneficiaries and applicants of irrevocable documentary credits.)
4 Bolero electronic bills of lading will be used to replace the present paper version. Bills of lading will be registered by Bolero on a central registry which will maintain a record of who are the holders of such bills. Thus no amendments or alterations can be made to this critical document without being registered by an authorized user.

Advantages

The advantages are obvious and have been spelt out earlier. Suffice it to say that on paper they appear to outweigh the disadvantages.

Disadvantages

Any scheme which sets out to replace a time-honoured document of title (The bill of lading) faces problems. One only has to consider the remarkable properties of a bill of lading to realise the difficulties arising from using its replacement.

The traditional bill of lading

1 A receipt for goods.
2 A contract of carriage.
3 A fully negotiable document of title.
4 A means of transferring title by simple endorsement.

Obviously banks and importers, used to the security and flexibility of the bill of lading, will be looking for something pretty sophisticated as an acceptable substitute. Where documents are perfectly in order and can be transmitted electronically to negotiating and issuing banks, those parties as *authorized users* can transfer title to the relevant goods *through the central registry.*

The Bolero bill of lading will show a *named consignee*, almost invariably the importer. The shipper can vary the identity of the consignee at any stage in the voyage provided he has not renounced that right when having his documents negotiated or collected by a bank. The obvious danger here lies in the possibility of the documents being subsequently refused for discrepancies not found at the time of negotiation/collection, leaving the shipper with no title and the importer with the *apparent* ability to get his goods without paying.

The authors of Bolero understandably signify their concern with the title aspects of the electronic bill of lading and are still considering means of perfecting title, but like it or not EDI will ensure that Bolero or its equivalent will eventually come into operation.

Chapter 12

Prevention of fraud in international trade

Experience has shown that fraud in international trade is invariably well-planned; it is rarely opportunistic and is often the result of collaboration between the beneficiary and the applicant. It takes a variety of forms: forged documents, fictitious shipments (phantom ships), alterations to genuine documents, shipment of sub-standard goods, chartering unseaworthy vessels, misuse of advance payments, and simultaneous presentations under one documentary credit to two or more negotiating banks are all examples of how unscrupulous operators attempt to perpetrate fraud.

What measures can be taken to minimize the risk of fraud?

Documentary credits

To consider this aspect of documentary credit use, we have to look first at the **issuing bank**. This is where it all begins and, in creating an instrument intended to protect the applicant against the risks of pre-shipment payment and faulty documentation and provide the beneficiary with a conditional guarantee of payment, the issuing bank can open the door to fraudulent use of it by both applicant and beneficiary. Once it is issued, an irrevocable credit must run its full course.

What factors influence the willingness of a bank to issue an irrevocable credit?

1 Knowledge of its customer and length of their relationship.
2 Assessment of the transaction covered by the credit:
    i   is it within the applicant's normal range of business?
    ii   if not, what is his motive for considering it?
    iii is he the end-user of the goods?
    iv if not, who is and how will he be paid?
    v   is a commodity involved and is it liable to excessive price fluctuation?
    vi who is the beneficiary?
    vii has the issuing bank dealt with the beneficiary before?
    viii are documents of title involved?
    ix is any form of pre-shipment finance stipulated?

Access to up-to-date information on all parties to any transaction is readily and swiftly available to banks and to protect themselves they must always make maximum use of those facilities.

Interpretation of applicants' mandates

The issuing bank must be certain that it has correctly followed its customer's instructions, but where such instructions are either unclear or threaten the bank's security they must be challenged immediately.

This scrutiny will be particularly applicable to:

- the structure of credits
- title to the goods
- pre-shipment finance
- the use of deferred payment credits
- transferable credits
- any deviation from UCP600 or ISP98
- the acceptance of electronically produced documents.

The advising bank. Although the responsibilities of the advising bank are limited to merely 'authenticating' an inward credit and therefore not concerning itself with the full details, it should not allow itself to remain silent when it 'smells a rat'.

For example, the beneficiary of a large credit may be quite unknown to the advising bank or not known for the type of transaction involved; a simple enquiry may reveal that the beneficiary is not an exporter.

There are those who will say that as there is no contractual relationship between the issuing bank and the advising bank it is of no concern to the latter if there are unusual aspects of the transaction. The response to them should be that all banks are at some time either issuers, advisers, confirmers, negotiators or reimbursers and they must be prepared to assist one another in the fight against fraud. The advising bank may well subsequently be asked to negotiate documents in circumstances which a little previous investigation might have prevented.

The confirming bank. As we know, assumes all the responsibilities of an issuing bank and as such must pay particular attention to the type of credit and the standing (track record) of the beneficiary. In addition it must ensure that it:

- adheres strictly to the credit terms
- understands the underlying transaction
- ensures title to the goods, where possible
- controls any pre-shipment finance
- correctly handles any discrepant documents
- protects reimbursement arrangements for transferable and back-to-back credits.

The reader will readily understand that considerable thought is necessary in order to calculate the risks involved if the credit is usance, transferable, deferred payment or provides for pre-shipment finance.

The negotiating, paying or accepting bank. Negotiation is generally the point at which fraud is crystallized, i.e. funds may be irretrievably paid away.

Negotiation carries the highest risk of all documentary credit operations and almost certainly accounts for the frequent reluctance of banks to adhere strictly to UCP600 (Article 12). Negotiating banks have to balance the desire to provide smooth and safe settlement of international trading transactions with the need to protect themselves against fraud.

How many of us have had serious doubts about a set of documents which, if paid, could result in our bank incurring a loss? Better safe than sorry!

Banks being asked to negotiate documents against credits pay special attention to bill of lading details, especially date of shipment, quality of shipping company, existence of nominated bank and confirming bank. The length of voyage is important, particularly when bills of lading may not reach the issuing bank before the vessel arrives. Banks are cautious about the seaworthiness of vessels (if chartered) and the age of vessels, often placing a limit of 15 years on them.

A number of sources are available to banks concerning shipping companies, vessels' itineraries, ages of vessels, etc; reference to them can often prevent a fraud being carried out.

It is essential that the negotiating bank forwards documents to the issuing bank in the manner stipulated in the credit, that it properly handles discrepant documents and that it carefully checks the validities of any advance payment bonds it may hold against advances made.

The expiry date of any bond should allow the negotiating bank at least 7 days after expiry of the relative credit, in case documents are out of order.

Banks operate documentary credits for the benefit of international trade and in so doing they assume considerable risks. They should not be coy about referring to one another, particularly when they sense trouble, although sometimes they seem reluctant to air their problems. Undoubtedly, banks with extensive branch networks benefit considerably from the exchange of valuable information and cautionary advice.

A particularly sensitive area in the use of documentary credits is the provision of pre-shipment finance through red clause, green clause and advance payment bond credits. There should be a positive reason for the beneficiary requiring an advance payment and advances should only be permitted between exporters and importers with established relationships or of undoubted standing. This may mean that, initially, advances are only made against some sort of security until the issuing bank has developed experience and knowledge of the parties involved and understands the underlying transactions.

Transferable and back-to-back credits often present the advising or confirming bank with the need to make a decision as to whether or not it wishes to either transfer a credit or establish a back-to-back credit. In this situation, the bank is being asked to accept instructions from the beneficiary of the prime credit who may be completely unknown to it. Does it wish to treat that beneficiary as a customer of the bank?

Banks are naturally cautious in their approach to transferable credits, and if we consider the cycle of such a credit we will see that the issuing bank can have no knowledge of the eventual transferee. Consequently it must assume that the transferee will behave in exactly the same way as the prime beneficiary, who is really a middleman and will supply exactly the goods described in the credit.

On occasions, an issuing bank may be asked by its customer to establish an irrevocable credit in which a third party is to be shown as the applicant, instead of the bank's customer. The explanations for such requests are usually genuine; for example, Company A may have entered into a contract for the purchase of certain goods, but because it has no banking facilities for opening credits, transfers the contract to its associate Company B which has those facilities.

The issuing bank must exercise caution in this situation and ask the third party applicant to complete a letter of authority on the lines of the specimen shown in Figure 12.1.

If the practice continues, the issuing bank should consider arranging facilities in the name of the third party applicant provided, of course, the credit risk is acceptable.

To . . . . Bank

By this letter, we, (Third Party):

(a) Irrevocably authorize you to comply with instructions given to you by (Client) in
our name for the opening, amendment and operation of a documentary letter of
credit as detailed below:

   L/C No . . . .
   Amount . . . .
   Beneficiary . . . .
   Goods . . . .

(b) Irrevocably authorize you to unconditionally endorse any Bills of Lading tendered
under the above documentary letter of credit exclusively as (Client) shall direct upon
the taking up of documents presented thereunder and release the said documents
to the order of (Client)

(c) Agree to ratify and confirm all acts carried out by you in conformity with the above
authorities.

Your acceptance of this statement is confirmation that you may make demand on (Client)
for payment under the above mentioned documentary letter of credit. (Third Party) shall
not be responsible for any claim of costs arising directly from (Client's) default relating to
the opening, amendment or operation of the credit and shall remain harmless from any
damage, claim, dispute or legal action due to (Client's) non-payment to the non-fulfilment
of our instructions.

This irrevocable authority is subject to and shall be construed in accordance with
. . . . Law.

Figure 12.1 Specimen letter of authority from third party applicant for a
documentary credit

The reason behind this suggested procedure lies in the important question
of title to goods. The bank, at some stage of a documentary credit will
assume title to the goods and will pay their value to the beneficiary. But,
even if the 'applicant' does have a title to the goods, he may not have the
right to dispose of the proceeds of their sale. It is possible that a charge may
exist on the 'applicant's' assets and if the issuing bank is unaware of this, it
is liable to an action for conversion.

For example, buyer A may purchase goods from seller B financed by a
documentary credit opened by an associate company C but showing A as
the applicant. The bank pays seller B, and buyer A on-sells the goods to final
buyer D. The proceeds of the sale to D is a 'receivable' in A's books and as

such belongs to whoever may have placed the charge on A's assets. As a consequence, in law, the bank has no right to the proceeds from D, with which it expects to reimburse itself for the payment it made to seller B under the documentary credit.

Standby credits and on-demand guarantees. These instruments are invariably payable on simple application by the beneficiary, raising the possibility of fraudulent claims. Collusion between the financial debtor and the beneficiary can make it extremely difficult to detect fraud under on-demand instruments. The issuing bank is responsible for:

■ wording
■ validity and automatic amendments
■ checking purpose – why standby and not documentary L/C?
■ reimbursement and place of payment
■ applying ISP98 and URDG
■ specifying applicable law
■ ensuring that when its guarantee is re-issued by a correspondent bank, the two instruments are identical.

Collections. Although banks handling collections are not themselves issuing instruments which provide payment for a third party, they are acting on instructions from the customer in obtaining payment for exports. Consequently, they must be aware of the possibility of fraud.

The remitting bank. This bank is responsible for:

■ scrutinizing large items
■ verifying shipping details – carrying vessel and whereabouts
■ ascertaining transaction is within exporter's normal area of trade
■ making advances where proceeds are to be directed back to remitting bank
■ exercising caution where customer requests right to forward collection direct to collecting bank
■ monitoring return of collection proceeds
■ protecting goods in accordance with exporter's instructions
■ noting D/A collections in excess of 60 days

The collecting bank. The collecting bank actually handles the proceeds of sight collections and is obliged to disperse them exactly in the manner stipulated by the remitting bank. It is responsible for:

- checking details of large items, carrying vessel, port of destination and ETA
- monitoring finance accorded to importers and sources of repayment
- monitoring D/A collections, especially when usance exceeds 60 days
- exercising care in dealing with a case of need (possible collusion with exporter).

The foregoing demonstrates the burden that fraud and money laundering place on banks engaged in trade finance; they deserve considerable sympathy! The penalties they face if they fail to detect illegal activity in any transaction can be severe. But the law is unremitting and expects a high level of vigilance from banks. In Agip (Africa) Ltd v. Jackson, 1990 it was stated:

> 'if a man does not draw obvious inferences or make the obvious enquiries, the question is, why not? If it is because, however foolishly, he did not suspect wrongdoing . . . that is one thing. But if he did suspect wrongdoing, yet failed to make enquiries because "he did not know" . . . or because he regarded it as "none of his business" . . . that is quite another. Such conduct is dishonest and those who are guilty of it cannot complain if, for the purpose of civil liability, they are treated as if they had actual knowledge.'
>
> Lloyds Law Reports

Appendix 1

Trade finance quiz

Q1   What does FOB mean?
      Who pays the freight?
Q2   What basic documents must be supplied for a CIF Shipment?
Q3   When documents are sent for collection on a D/A basis, when are they
      released to the importer?
Q4   How would you describe a clean bill of lading?
Q5   Name three types of credits which provide pre-shipment finance.
Q6   Who makes the first presentation under a transferable credit?
Q7   You are the advising bank for a $250 000 credit valid for 9 months.
      The issuing bank asks you to confirm the credit. Are you obliged
      to:
      (a) confirm it?
      (b) confirm it for 9 months?
      (c) confirm it for $250 000?
Q8   As an exporter you are offered by the importer:
      (a) a usance credit
      (b) a deferred payment credit.
          Which would you prefer and why?
Q9   What is the purpose of a tender bond?
Q10 Does a mate's receipt give title to the goods detailed on it?
Q11 There are three parties appearing on the front of a bill of exchange,
      who are they? Could there be more than three parties to the bill? If
      so, how?

Q12 A buyer in Turkey buys three combine harvesters from an exporter in Paris on ex works terms for shipment to Izmir – list the costs to be borne by the buyer.

Q13 What does 'pour aval' mean when applied to a bill of exchange?

Q14 What is a multimodal bill of lading? If it is to be acceptable under a documentary credit, what essential feature must it have?

Q15 Why do we call a standby credit a negative credit? How did this type of credit originate?

Q16 You are an exporter selling goods on a collection basis. If you sold FOB or CFR, would you be taking a greater risk than selling CIF?

Q17 Uniform Rules for Collection require the collecting bank to advise the remitting bank immediately upon non-payment or non-acceptance by the drawee – why?
Sometimes the remitting bank asks to be advised immediately upon payment – why?

Q18 Documents for a value of US$150 000 are presented against a CIF credit. They include an insurance certificate for £100 000. The current exchange rage is US$1.50 = £1. Is the insurance certificate acceptable?

Q19 An irrevocable credit is opened covering 6000 tons of steel; part shipments are not permitted. What is the minimum quantity the exporter may ship in accordance with UCP600?

Q20 Who can sign a bill of lading?

Q21 What is the difference between a shipping company's bill of lading and a charterparty bill of lading?

Q22 (a) What is the difference between a bill of exchange drawn at 90 days fixed and one drawn at 90 days sight?
(b) As a negotiating bank, which would you prefer if the drawee was in a foreign country?

Q23 What must the drawee do to become liable on a bill of exchange?

Q24 The beneficiary of a transferable credit requests the nominated bank to transfer it. What alterations is he permitted to make under UCP600?

Q25 If a credit calls for a 'shipped' bill of lading, what would you look for to ensure that the bill of lading presented was correct?

Q26 You are the issuing bank and you receive documents under one of your credits from a negotiating bank. Upon examination you discover discrepancies. Who do you contact first:

(a) the applicant, or

(b) the negotiating bank?

How much time do you have according to UCP600?

Q27 Documents are presented under a credit covering shipment of six cases of machine tools. What particular detail, which will appear on all documents, must be identical on each?

Q28 Under what circumstances would a remitting bank examine documents which it was handling as a collection?

Q29 You receive from the issuing bank, a red clause credit which you advise to the beneficiary. The credit allows a cash advance of 20%:

(a) Are you obliged to make the advance?

(b) Would it make any difference if you have confirmed the credit?

Q30 Name two negotiable instruments.

Q31 What is the difference between an offset deal and a counterpurchase deal?

Q32 Are switch currencies convertible?

Q33 Under countertrade deals what is the original supplier committed to do?

Q34 What is the term used to describe a deal set up solely for the exchange of goods?

Q35 What do you understand by the term compensation when applied to a countertrade deal?

Appendix 2

Guide to exporters and importers

In all international trade transactions, much depends on the relationship between buyer and seller. Put simply, the higher the level of trust between buyer and seller, the lower the risk of default, and consequently the cheaper the bank product.

Exporters

How well do you know your buyer?
Have you any experience of exporting to his country?
Have you obtained bank reports on him?

If you are still not 100% confident that you buyer is undoubted and will meet his obligation, you should insist that the contract between you stipulates payment by one of the following methods:

- documentary collection
- irrevocable documentary credit
- confirmed irrevocable documentary credit
- standby credit.

By using one of those methods of settlement you can reduce or eliminate the main risks:

1 Commercial: non-payment or delayed payment by importer.
2 Political:
   - non-release of foreign exchange in buyer's country
   - failure by issuing bank to pay

What cover do those methods provide?

Bill for collection:

- non-payment is **not** covered
- non release of foreign exchange is **not** covered.

But the collection does have certain attractions:

- it is simple and cheap
- it ensures that the buyer cannot obtain your goods until he has either paid cash or has accepted a bill of exchange
- it provides a means of obtaining post-shipment finance.

Put simply, the exporter entrusts his shipping documents to a bank (remitting bank) which undertakes to send them to a collecting bank in the buyer's country with instructions as to how that bank should present them to the buyer for payment.

There are two types of documentary collections:

D/P: documents only to be released against payment.
D/A: documents to be released against acceptance by the buyer of a bill of exchange payable at a future date.

Obviously, D/A carries greater risks than D/P because once the buyer has accepted a bill of exchange, he can take the documents of title, obtain release of the goods and may eventually fail to meet the bill of exchange at maturity.

Exporters should therefore be extremely careful before agreeing to payment by D/A collection.

Some protection against non-payment of a D/A Collection can be obtained by having the bill of exchange 'avalised' (guaranteed) by a bank in the buyer's country after acceptance by him.

Exporters' instructions to remitting bank

To avoid problems arising through non-payment, non-acceptance, late payment, etc., exporters should make clear in their instructions:

- in the event of non-payment whether they wish the relative goods to be warehoused and insured
- whether documents may be released to the buyer even if he refuses to pay the collecting bank's charges
- what is to happen to the bill of exchange after it has been accepted (discount, etc.)
- how proceeds of the collection are to be remitted back.

Additionally, it is extremely helpful if the exporter has a contact in the buyer's country to whom the collecting bank can refer if they experience difficulties.

This contact is called a '**case of need**'.

Irrevocable documentary credits

As previously stated, all contracts between buyer and seller should stipulate the method of settlement, and if that method is by irrevocable credit then the contract should be clear and concise as to:

- whether documentary credits should be confirmed or unconfirmed, sight or usance
- exact type required, e.g. straight, negotiation, revolving, red clause, etc.
- documentation required; this is particularly important where the applicant is not the actual importer, but simply a merchant selling the goods on to an importer possibly in another country
- description of goods (possibly the most critical factor in irregular documents), the quantity and the unit price
- period allowed for shipment and validity of the credit.

What cover against risks does the irrevocable credit give the exporter?

1 The credit contains an undertaking by the issuing bank that, provided the beneficiary (exporter) complies with all its terms and presents documents in order within the validity date, **he will be paid**, thus he does not have to worry about his buyer's ability to pay.
2 Once issued, the credit is available until expiry; cancellation can only be made with the agreement of all parties.

However, the irrevocable credit does not protect the exporter against the possibility that although the buyer may accept the documents and pay in his **local currency**, the central bank may refuse to release the foreign exchange or the issuing bank may not be able to pay. This is known as the **sovereign risk** or **political risk**. To obtain protection against that risk the exporter can ask for the credit to be **confirmed** by the bank in his own country.

Once confirmed, the credit will be paid even if the issuing bank does not reimburse the confirming bank.

Confirmation is not cheap and exporters should think carefully before they demand it; the charges are usually down to them.

Generally speaking, credits issued by most large international banks (e.g. Credit Agricole Indosuez, HK&S, Citibank, Deutsche Bank, etc.) do not need confirming.

General observations for exporters using documentary credits

When advice of the credit is received:

1 Check that validity and latest shipment dates can be met.
2 Check required documentation and request amendment from the applicant if you cannot comply. For example, legalization of invoices or certificate of origin may be impossible in your town/city of business.
3 If the issuing bank is unknown to you, ask the advising bank to provide details of their standing.

4 If their standing does not satisfy you, ask the advising bank to add their confirmation to the letter of credit. (**Remember**, you may have to pay the charges!)

5 Diarize the latest shipment and expiry dates, especially if you are producing or manufacturing goods. If you miss the latest shipment date you are entirely at the mercy of the applicant who may either:

 ■ agree to extend by asking for a price reduction
 ■ refuse to extend because the market has moved in his favour and he can purchase the same goods more cheaply elsewhere.

6 Make certain that you present all the required documents when requesting negotiation under the credit and ensure that they are in full compliance with the terms.

7 If the negotiating bank refuses your documents due to a discrepancy(ies):

 ■ ask for them back and correct the discrepancy(ies), or
 ■ request the negotiating bank to telex the issuing bank for authority to pay, or
 ■ ask for the documents to be sent to the issuing bank for applicant's approval, or
 ■ ask for them to be sent on a collection basis under the letter of credit and within the terms of UCP600 (this usually happens when the discrepancies are too serious to rectify).

Remember that all discrepant documents belong to you until the applicant agrees to take them up.

If he signifies to the issuing bank that he will not accept them, he cannot subsequently change his mind and accept them **without your approval**. The reason is obvious: you may, in the meantime, have found an alternative buyer and agreed to sell him the underlying goods.

What other benefits can an exporter derive from an irrevocable credit?

1 Advance payments: credits can be structured to permit the beneficiary (exporter) to draw an advance of say 20% for expenses/charges, etc.,

incurred in manufacturing/procuring raw materials, etc. Such advances are a feature of:

- red clause credits
- green clause credits
- advance payment credits: advances payable against APBs (advance payment bonds).

2 The ability to use a credit as a means of purchasing the goods required under it. To do this, the exporter should ask his buyer to open a transferable credit. A transferable credit allows the beneficiary to transfer it, on identical terms, to his own supplier.

Example

Buyer A in London issues a transferable credit in favour of seller B in Dhaka for US$75 000.

Seller B in Dhaka transfers that credit to seller C in Bombay for US$69 500. Seller C is paid US$69 500 in Bombay by the Dhaka bank who pay seller B US$5 500 and claim US$75 000 from the London bank.

Similarly, and for established and undoubted customers, banks will consider opening back-to-back credits using an inward credit as security.

Example

Buyer A in London opens a credit in favour of seller B in Dhaka for US$75 000 (this credit is **not transferable**).

The Dhaka bank receiving the credit from London, agrees with seller B to open a back-to-back credit in favour of seller C in Bombay for US$69 500.

From then on, the credit operates like a transferable credit **but** the ICC Uniform Customs and Practice (600) does not recognize back-to-back credits and banks have to be extremely careful issuing them.

Standby credits

The standby credit is comparatively young compared with the documentary credit and is distinguishable by the fact that it does not require presentation of shipping documents.

It is what we call a **negative** credit, i.e. it is payable when someone **fails** to do something, whereas a documentary credit is payable when someone **does** something (ships goods, presents documents).

How does the standby credit work?

Example

Seller A in Dhaka ships goods every month to buyer B in Paris for which he is paid against irrevocable documentary credits. Buyer B says 'look, you know you have always been paid every month and these documentary credits are tying up my bank facilities. I will open, in your favour, a standby credit covering the value of 2 months' shipments and we will then trade on open account. You send me your shipping documents direct each month and I will transfer the payment to you in Dhaka. The standby credit will allow payment against your letter stating that I have not paid you for a previous month's shipment, so that, immediately I fail to pay, you can claim under the credit. You then have the choice to stop sending me goods or demand a documentary credit'.

The standby credit is widely used in the United States where banks are prohibited by law from issuing guarantees.

International Standby Practices ISP98 has recently been introduced by the ICC to provide separate rules for this instrument, which has proved difficult to comply with UCP600 (documentary credits).

In view of the close similarity between the standby and 'on-demand' bank guarantees, you are strongly advised to discuss with you bank which is the best applicable to the transaction you wish to cover.

Importers

How well do you know your overseas suppliers? Are you certain that:

- they will fully comply with the terms of your contract with them?
- they will complete delivery of the required goods within the prescribed time allowed?
- they will deliver goods of perfect quality?
- they will not request advance payments without offering acceptable security?

Strict adherence to contract terms is of the utmost importance to you, especially if you are on-selling to a buyer to whom you are also contracted.

The following products will enable you to considerably reduce the risk of default by your supplier:

- irrevocable documentary credit
- advance payment bond
- performance bond
- retention bond.

The irrevocable documentary credit

- Will ensure that your supplier cannot be paid until he produces and presents the documents stipulated in the credit.

- Will ensure that your supplier cannot be paid if those documents are out of order.

- Can include documents which will evidence that the goods are as described in the buyer/seller contract, e.g. independent inspection report.

- Can be payable against documents which include a **performance bond** issued by a bank acceptable to the issuing bank.

- Can permit advance payment(s) against suitable security, e.g. bankers advance payment bond, warehouse warrant (approved warehouse).

■ Can be payable as to, say, 85% against shipping documents with a balance of 15% payable after independent inspection **at port of destination**.

If your supplier is not prepared to wait for payment of the 15% balance, it can be 100% provided he presents, with his shipping documents, a **retention bond** issued by a bank acceptable to the issuing bank.

■ Can be payable at a future determinable date, thus allowing you to obtain credit from your supplier, i.e. it can be payable 30/60/90/180 days from presentation of documents and is known as a usance or term credit.

These credits are particularly useful when importers are selling on to buyers who, in turn, demand credit.

General points to be observed by importers

1 If your contract does not state specifically the terms of the credit, you should have it opened as you think appropriate and leave your supplier to accept or reject it.
2 You may send a pre-advice of the credit, but if you do so through your bank make sure that it is sent 'without engagement' otherwise the bank will be obliged to issue the full credit subsequently.
3 Where the contract does not specify the terms of the credit, any subsequent agreement between the two parties as to its terms following issue by the applicant's bank may be said to supplement the contract of sale (Shamsher Jute Mills Ltd v. Sethia (London) Ltd, 1987).
4 You are strongly advised **not** to include contract details in your documentary credit applications. The reason is obvious: if you amend the terms of your contract with the exporter, the credit will also require amendment if it contains contract details. If you should overlook or delay the credit amendment, the beneficiary will be obliged to present his documents in accordance with its **original** terms, otherwise the negotiating bank will refuse to pay him.
5 It can be made available to a supplier anywhere in the world, in any currency.
6 If your supplier asks for a **confirmed irrevocable credit** make sure that your issuing bank stipulates that confirmation charges are for account of the beneficiary (your supplier) – they can be high!

7 Remember, if you are importing goods under an irrevocable credit and intend selling those goods on to a final buyer, the issuing bank will either want you to pay immediately you take up the documents or will need some form of security to ensure it is paid by your buyer.

If your supplier demands that you open a standby credit in his favour, you should be extremely careful.

The standby credit requires **no documents** except a written claim by your supplier stating that you have not paid for a certain delivery. The risks are obvious:

- he could make a false claim
- you have no negotiating bank, who will ensure that the import documents you require are absolutely correct or will refuse to pay the supplier until you approve the documents.

Appendix 3

Suggested checklist for beneficiaries when preparing documents for presentation under a documentary credit

1 Is credit still valid?
2 Is the available balance sufficient to cover presentation?
3 Is the draft to be drawn on issuing or confirming bank?
4 Is the draft drawn correctly and for the tenor stipulated in the credit?
5 Is the invoice issued by you and is your name shown exactly as stated in the credit?
6 Does the invoice agree with supporting documents as regards unit price, description of goods, weight and term of shipment?
7 Where documents include shipping marks, are they exactly as shown on the document of despatch?
8 Has the invoice or certificate of origin been certified and/or legalized if required under the credit terms?
9 Are miscellaneous documents, such as packing list, inspection certificate, weight note, etc., issued separately and not combined with other documents?
10 Are all documents issued by the parties stipulated in the credit?
11 Is the insurance document issued for the correct percentage of cover, usually 10% above CIF value and is it in the same currency as the credit?

12 Is the insurance document dated no later than the transport document?

13 Does it show the name of the agent responsible for handling claims and is it properly endorsed?

14 Is a full set of bills of lading being presented? If not, does the credit allow an original to go direct to consignee?

15 Are the bills of lading stamped 'freight paid' or 'freight payable at destination' as stipulated in the credit? Are they properly issued and endorsed?

16 Do the bills of lading show a 'notify' party?

17 If the bill of lading is a charterparty bill, does the credit allow it?

Appendix 4

Answers to Gdanski Construct SA Case Study

1 Gdanski Construct SA, if successful with their bid will be supplying materials to and carrying out work for a foreign buyer. Their initial risks are:-
   - Financial
   - Political
   - Foreign exchange

   Financial risks
   (a) non-payment by Combinex for materials
   (b) non-payment by Combinex for construction.

   Political risks
   (a) refusal by Canadian Central Bank to release foreign exchange
   (b) embargo by Canadian Government on import of steel products
   (c) refusal by Canadian Government to grant work permits to Polish construction force.

   Foreign exchange risks
   (a) adverse movement between the Can. $ and Zloty before advance payments are made
   (b) adverse movement between the Can. $ and Zloty for stage payments, completion and acceptance payments
   (c) adverse movement between the Can. $ and Zloty for four promissory notes maturing over a period of 4 years.

2 Gdanski Construct SA will need the following instruments to cover the risks inherent in this contract:

  1 Confirmed irrevocable documentary credit from Combinex bankers to cover shipments of materials.
  2 Confirmed standby credit to cover possibility of failure by Combinex to make stage payments.
  3 Confirmed standby credit to cover completion and acceptance payments.
  4 Endorsement by approved bank on each promissory note guaranteeing payment at maturity.
  5 Forward exchange contracts or currency options to protect against exchange movements.

3 Combinex Inc. face the following risks in conducting this contract with a foreign supplier:
  • Financial
  • Political
  • Foreign exchange

  Financial risks
  (a) non-refund by Gdanski Construct of advance payments of 10% (materials) and 10% (construction)
  (b) failure by Gdanski Construct to supply materials and to complete construction in accordance with contract
  (c) supply of sub-standard materials.
  Political
  (a) refusal of Polish Central Bank to release funds if advance payments have to be repaid
  (b) embargo on export of steel products by Polish Government
  (c) refusal by Canadian Government to grant work permits to Polish construction force.

  Foreign exchange
  (a) adverse movement between Can. $ and Zloty before advance payments are made
  (b) adverse movement between Can. $ and Zloty before stage payments, completion and acceptance payments are made

(c) adverse movement between Can. $ and Zloty during the life of four promissory notes.

4 Combinex will require the following measures to cover their risks:
  1 Advance payment bonds from an acceptable bank for 10% of value of materials and construction work.
  2 Performance bond from acceptable bank for 10% of contract value covering construction, quality of materials and standard of work.
  3 Forward exchange contracts, with options, for advance payments.
  4 Forward exchange contracts for stage payments, completion and acceptance payments.

5 Forward exchange contracts to cover maturities of four promissory notes.

Alternatively, currency options could be used for 3, 4 and 5.

Appendix 5

Answers to Quiz

1 Free on board.
  The importer.
2 Invoice.
  Freight paid bill of lading.
  Insurance document.
3 Upon acceptance of the bill of exchange.
4 One that bears no superimposed clause which declares a defective condition of the goods and/or packaging.
5 Red clause credit.
  Green clause credit.
  Advance payment credit requiring beneficiary to provide an advance payment bond.
6 The transferee.
7 (a) No.
  (b) No.
  (c) No.
8 The usance credit, as it requires a bill of exchange which is discountable, whereas the deferred payment credit has no bill of exchange and the letter of undertaking is not discountable.
9 To demonstrate that the tender is made in good faith and with intent to proceed if successful.
10 No – it is eventually released against a bill of lading.

11 (a) Drawer, drawee, payee.

(b) Yes, the acceptor may be a bank accepting on behalf of the drawee.

12 Transport to port of shipment.

Ocean freight.

Transport from port of destination.

Insurance.

13 Payment guaranteed.

14 One covering two or more modes of transport. To be acceptable under a documentary credit this document must cover at least one sea journey.

15 It is payable when one party, usually the applicant, fails to carry out an obligation and originated in the US where banks are forbidden by law to issue on-demand guarantees.

16 Yes, you would be liable to pay freight and insurance in a foreign currency and would therefore face an exchange risk.

17 (a) To alert the exporter and enable him to discontinue despatching goods until reasons for default are known.

(b) To enable the exporter to sell the foreign exchange.

18 No, insurance must be for US$165 000 (CIF value +10%) and the insurance document must be in the same currency as the credit.

19 6000 tons less 5% (5700 tons): Article 30.

20 (a) The carrier or a named agent for or on behalf of the carrier.

(b) The master or a named agent for or on behalf of the master.

21 A shipping company bill of lading covers the goods from a named port of shipment to a named port of destination whereas a charterparty bill of lading enables the charterer to deliver the cargo to any destination he may choose.

22 (a) (i) The fixed bill is payable 90 days from its date of issue.

(ii) The sight bill is payable 90 days from the date on which it is sighted.

(b) The fixed bill.

23 Accept it.

24 He may alter: amount, price, validity, latest shipment date, name of applicant and percentage margin over C.I.F value.

25 It evidences shipment *on board*.

26 (a) The applicant.

(b) Seven days maximum.

27 Shipping marks.

28 When it had a financial interest in the collection, i.e. it had advanced against it.

29 (a) No.

(b) Yes, the advance payment would then be obligatory.

30 Bill of exchange.

Promissory note.

31 Offset deals are settled by purchase of goods from the importing country by the exporter; *no foreign exchange is involved*. Counterpurchase deals are simply agreements whereby two countries export goods to each other for a maximum amount and over a fixed period. *All settlements are made in foreign exchange.*

32 No, they can only be used to purchase goods or can be sold to a specialist dealer.

33 Undertake to purchase goods from the importing country.

34 Barter.

35 Settlement by the importer in part foreign exchange and part goods.

Glossary

Applicant   The party instructing a bank to issue a documentary credit.

Assignment   Transfer of rights to proceeds of a credit.

Aval   Bank guarantee of payment endorsed on reverse of bill of exchange.

Back-to-back credit   A documentary credit supported by a prime credit on identical terms.

Beneficiary   The party to whom a documentary credit is addressed and who is entitled to eventual payment.

Bill of lading   A receipt issued by a carrier for goods consigned by sea and detailing terms of carriage.

Case of need   Drawers' agent appointed to assist in event of non-payment of a collection.

Charterparty   Contract of hire between vessel owner and shipper.

Collection   Method of presenting documents to an overseas buyer for payment or acceptance.

Confirming bank   Any bank which adds its own undertaking to another bank's credit.

Consignee   Party to whom goods are despatched.

Days of grace   Describes a fee charged by a forfaiter to compensate for loss of interest due to transfer and deliver delays.

Deferred payment   Payment under an irrevocable credit which is deferred until a fixed future date and requires no bill of exchange.

Demurrage   A charge raised for detaining a vessel at a port beyond its intended stay.

Discount   The purchase at sight of a term bill of exchange.

Discount margin The difference between the fixed interest rate charged for discounting and the true discount to yield rate.

Documentary credit An instrument issued by a bank on the instruction of the applicant by which a third party, the beneficiary, may receive payment for specified documents.

Draft An alternative description of a bill of exchange.

Embargo Government ban on import or export of certain goods.

Endorsement Signature placed on reverse of bill of exchange with intent to transfer title.

Freely negotiable Description of a credit available for negotiation with any bank.

Freight forwarder The agent of an exporter or importer who arranges carriage to and from ports of shipment and destination.

Green clause credit A documentary credit which allows an advance payment against acceptable security.

Guarantee An undertaking given by one party to be responsible for the debt of default of another.

Incoterms International rules for the interpretation of trade terms.

Injunction An order made by a court of law preventing a bank from meeting a demand for payment from a third party.

Irrevocable Description of a credit which cannot be cancelled without the agreement of all parties.

LIBOR London Interbank Offer Rate (interest).

Mate's receipt A receipt for goods awaiting shipment on a vessel; it is exchanged for bills of lading when the goods are loaded. It is not a document of title.

Margin Percentage deposit taken by some issuing banks by way of security for advances against collections and opening documentary credits.

Master credit The original credit in a back-to-back operation.

Maturity Date on which a term bill is payable.

Middleman Trader or merchant operating between original supplier and ultimate buyer.

Multimodal Description of a bill of lading covering two or more means of transport.

Negotiable Transferable by delivery or endorsement.

Nominated bank The bank selected by an issuing bank to advise its credit to the beneficiary.

Option   The right to take up or abandon a currency option.

Performance bond   An undertaking given by a bank to compensate a third party for the failure by its customer to carry out certain obligations.

Pledge   Authority given to a bank by a customer permitting the bank to handle title documents for its own account.

Receivables   Book debts due from overseas buyers.

Received for shipment bill of lading   A bill of lading issued as a receipt for goods awaiting loading.

Recourse   The right to reclaim payment from the party to whom it was made.

Red clause credit   A documentary credit which allows unsecured advances to be made.

Reimbursement   Settlement by a third party bank appointed to meet claims for negotiation under documentary credits.

Revocable credit   A documentary credit which may be cancelled without the need for agreement by the beneficiary.

Sight   Description of a bill of exchange payable on presentation.

Silent confirmation   Confirmation of an irrevocable credit made without the knowledge of the issuing bank.

SWIFT   Society for Worldwide Interbank Financial Telecommunications.

Tolerance   Allowances above and below quantities of goods shipped in bulk under UCP600.

Under reserve   A method of payment to the beneficiary under a documentary credit despite discrepancies in the documents; the beneficiary is obliged to refund such payment if the documents are ultimately refused by the issuing bank.

Usance   Describes an irrevocable credit payable against presentation of a term bill of exchange.

Voyage diversion   Re-routing of a vessel due to *force majeure*.

Waiver   Agreement by the applicant of a documentary credit to accept documents despite the existence of discrepancies.

Bibliography

I am indebted to Union de Banques Suisse for inspiration gained over many years of reading their *Guide to Documentary Transactions in Foreign Trade* and to my friends and colleagues in Credit Agricole Indosuez who provided a wide range of actual day-to-day operations and incidents experienced in their world-wide network.

Suggested reading

Jack, Raymond (1993) *Documentary Credits*. (By far the most lucid and accurate commentary on that complex instrument that I have read; compulsory reading for today's operators.)
Rowe, M. and Wickeremeratne, L. (2001) *The Complete Guide to Documentary Credits*. Financial World Publishing.
Todd, Paul (1998) *Bills of Lading and Bankers Documentary Credits*. Institute of Bankers.
Watson, A. (1981) *Finance of International Trade*. Institute of Bankers.

Index

Lightning Source UK Ltd.
Milton Keynes UK
22 October 2010

161687UK00003B/22/P